Hair & Wigs for the Stage

Rosemarie Swinfield

Hair & Wigs for the Stage

Step-by-Step

BETTERWAY BOOKS
Cincinnati, Ohio

Contents

*To the London College of Fashion
(then Barrett Street Technical College)
which gave a reluctant student a wonderful
grounding in hair and wig techniques.*

Acknowledgments

I would like to express my thanks to the following people and businesses for their invaluable help with this book ~

Marian Titchmarsh for yet again deciphering my terrible handwriting with such patience, Tesni Hollands and Katie Taylor for their editorial wisdom and Susan McIntyre for her brilliant design ideas and making the Key Tools look such fun. Brenda Needham of R.A.D.A. for her generous loan of period costumes, Derek Easton and Gary Curtis for the terrific wigs. Charles Fox and Screenface for loaning theatrical products and Capitol Hair & Beauty for the Key Tools. Wella and L'Oréal kindly lent us hair products for the photographs, which were taken by Colin Willoughby who always understands exactly what I need. Terry Harris again provided sterling support during the photoshoot achieving small miracles every day. Thanks also to Rodney Cottier of L.A.M.D.A. and all the models who worked so brilliantly in their characters for the photographs.

Front cover photograph of Margaret McEwan; wig styled by Gary Curtis.
Back cover photographs of Nikki Amuka-Bird, Robert Wallace, Lorna Bennett and Matthew Ghil.
Photographs taken by Colin Willoughby.
Photograph of Rosemarie Swinfield by Katie Vandyck.

First published in the USA in 1999 by
Betterway Books, an imprint of F&W Publications Inc.,
1507 Dana Avenue, Cincinnati, Ohio 45207, USA

© 1999 Text and charts Rosemarie Swinfield,
© Photographs A & C Black (Publishers) Limited

ISBN 1-55870-513-9

Originally published in 1999 by A & C Black (Publishers) Limited, 35 Bedford Row, London WC1R 4JH

A CIP catalog record for this book is available from the Library of Congress.

Typeset in 11 on 13pt Garamond Light

Printed in China through Colorcraft Ltd.

Introduction

Although I am firstly and foremost a make-up designer, over the years I have frequently found myself dealing with hair and wigs as well. It might be a photoshoot where the photographer would like the model's hair "tidied up a bit", or a stage production where wigs are needed and the wardrobe department has no experience of handling them, or a play set in the 1930s where the actresses need to set their own hair in period and don't know how to go about it.

So I bless my training in hair and wigs all those years ago at the London College of Fashion. At the time I did the hairdressing and wig-making part of my course with great reluctance and on leaving went straight to the Max Factor salon in Bond Street to learn make-up instead. But since then I have been so grateful for the excellent training I received there — it has stood me in great stead ever since.

When my publishers suggested that my next book should cover hairstyles and wigs, I decided to do some research, both here and in America, to see what was available already. To my surprise, I found that there didn't appear to be the sort of book that was needed — something that gave all the little tips which I have learned during my career and found so helpful. A book that isn't designed to turn you into a professional hairstylist or wig-dresser, but one which explains in simple basic terms how to deal with the myriad of hair and wig problems that confront actors, make-up designers and wardrobe depart-

ments in productions all the time. Things like attaching false pieces to your own hair, setting a period style, fixing false eyebrows on securely, and low budget options for wigs and facial hair.

So here is the book that I couldn't find. I have divided it into three sections — one for working with your own hair, one for wigs and false hair and a final section dealing with period styles. This last section complements my previous book *Period Make-up for the Stage* and shows you hairstyles and facial hair combined with the correct make-up of the time to give a complete picture.

On page 13 you will find a list of Key Tools that will help you to achieve perfect results every time. Most of them are widely available but a few come from specialist shops. A guide to hair products has been provided at the end of Section 1.

I have also included advice on how to deal with one of the most challenging things to use properly — the bald cap — since it is often associated with wigs as, for example, in Restoration plays. I hope you will find this an invaluable reference book for your work and that you will enjoy learning from it as well.

I suggest that you read through the section that you are working with before you actually begin so that, rather as with a cookery recipe, you don't find yourself at a vital point without a key tool.

Our models

Nikki Amuka-Bird,
pages 2,10, 49, 60, 61, 107, 108, 120, 122

Matthew Ghil,
pages 25, 26, 43, 44, 51, 79, 87, 91, 93

Lorna Bennett,
pages 26, 53, 86, 95, 112, 119

Stuart Murray,
pages 42, 109, 111

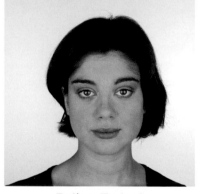

Rajère Ferjani,
pages 3, 11, 21, 32, 33, 40, 52, 58, 87, 102, 105

David Oyelowo,
page 42

Zena Khan,
pages 3, 35, 36, 37

Rosemary Denny,
pages 56, 105

Giles Fagan,
pages 42, 96, 103, 106, 117, 119, 121

Margaret McEwan,
pages 11, 25, 31, 49, 62, 63, 90

Robert Wallace,
pages 3, 42, 44, 48, 83, 84, 85, 121, 122

Sara Korsvnova,
pages 3, 54, 57, 92, 101, 116

Terry Harris,
pages 44, 59

Joanne Taylor,
pages 24, 55, 88, 110, 113, 115, 122

James Teacher,
pages 72, 74, 75, 99, 109, 117, 122

Fritha Goodey,
pages 98, 118

Chris Naylor,
pages 57, 91, 100, 114

Hair or wig?

When to use your own hair or wear a wig ~ some basic facts

For **men** this is a fairly simple decision:

• You may be able to adapt your own hair (see page 42 for possible uses of different hair lengths).

• If your hair is too short for your character or the period, you can either attempt to grow it to the required length or wear a wig.

• If your hair is too long, you can either get it cut to the correct style or wear a wig.

• If you are balding or your own hair is too thin for the style, you will need to wear a wig.

For **women** the decision is more complex. To help you to decide I have compared three different hair lengths to see what is possible with each of them.

Short hair

As you can see with our model here, there is very little that can be done in the way of restyling hair that is this short. Nine times out of ten a director will ask you to wear a wig. Occasionally one will let you use your own hair in a modern play, but that will be unusual. Even if you use a wig there will still be problems. Because the hair is very short, the usual way of covering it, with a wig net of some sort, is unnecessary. This means that the wig is directly over the natural hair and it will be tricky to secure with grips. You will need to attach wig springs to your hair to hold pins or grips and secure the wig (see page 60).

Mid-length hair

This length, which comes just below the ears, is much more versatile and can be styled in many ways and for a number of different periods.

For example, it can be dressed in a typical everyday 1970s style — backcombed on the top to give height and rolled under. Alternatively, this length could easily be set in a 1930s style.

It is also just long enough to be dressed into a French pleat (page 36) and could be set back to have a hairpiece added. With a stocking cap over it, this hair will go easily under most wigs.

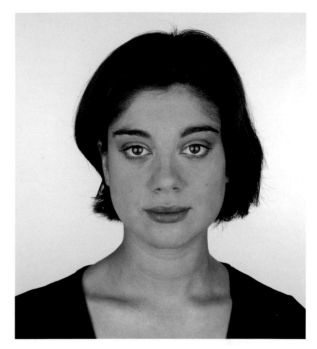

Long hair

This is the most versatile length in one sense because you can dress it up or wear it down. As long as you are reasonably good with hair you can create a variety of period styles. It will make a wonderful French pleat and can be curled into Victorian ringlets or set into 1940s styles with little problem.

Problems arise when long hair has to go underneath a wig — you cannot just push the hair under it or your head will look deformed. A special technique of wrapping the hair around the head will solve this problem (see page 62). Hair that is extremely long is much less versatile. Set styles are difficult to create if there is too much hair and it will also be hard to fit under most wigs.

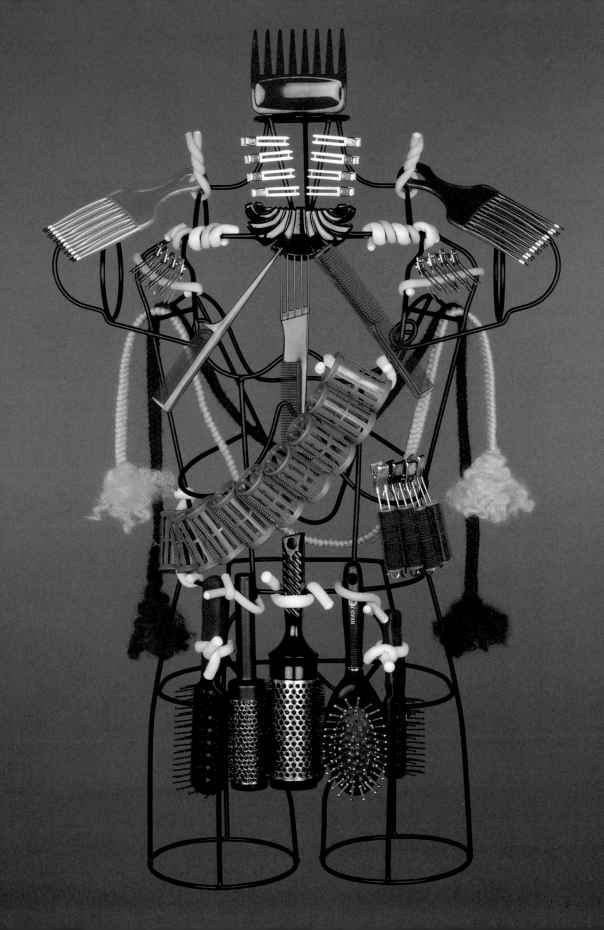

Key tools

A workman is, so they say, only as good as his tools and hair is certainly a lot easier to handle if you have the right equipment. Often when I have been helping actors, I have found that they simply don't have the right sort of brush or comb, enough hairpins or even hairspray, to achieve the style they need. You waste time with the wrong equipment, so I have compiled a list of Key Tools and what they are useful for when working with your own hair.

Brushes

There are many shapes and sizes but these are the most useful:

Typical hairbrush

This type is best for the initial brushing through of a set after removing rollers or hairclips. It needs to be firm, not soft, to brush through properly. It is also helpful for very thick or long hair. If you can afford it, choose a real bristle version. If not, look for one with rounded ends to the synthetic bristles, which will be kinder to your hair.

Roller brush

This is designed for blow-drying hair. Again look for bristles with rounded ends. These brushes come in different sizes and you choose the one appropriate for your needs. Remember, the smaller the brush you use, the tighter the finished curl will be, so it is important to select the right size. If, for example, you want a rather set look to the style, a large roller brush would be the wrong choice as it will give too soft a shape to the hair.

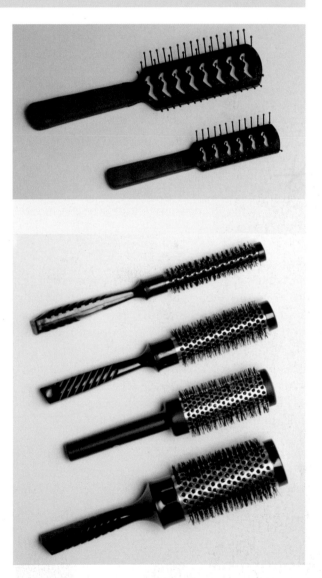

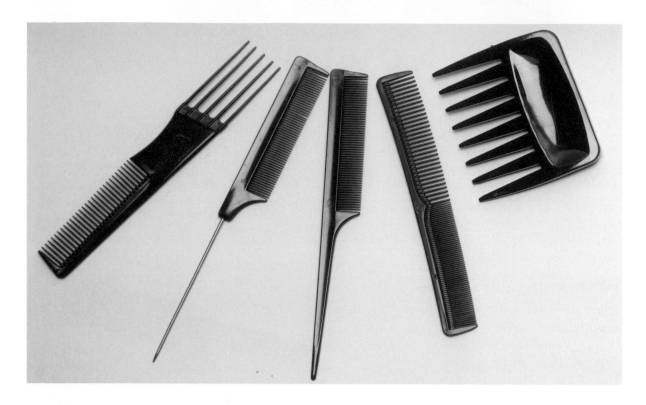

Combs

These come in all shapes and sizes, materials and colors.

Tail comb

This is a most useful comb. It is excellent for parting and sectioning hair (you use the long end for this, not the teeth), essential for back-combing or teasing, and wonderful for lifting the shape of a style after using hairspray. It is also useful for tucking stray hair back under wigs. A *must* for every actress! The metal-ended version is the best because the end is less likely to snap off.

Wide tooth comb

Only helpful for thick, curly hair where a narrow tooth comb will get caught and pull the hair.

Man's graduated comb

Really only useful for men. You can comb through with the wider tooth end and part with the narrow one.

Afro comb

Ideal for African-American and very curly hair. Useless for anything else.

Rollers

You need these to achieve set styles. Many types and sizes are available.

Metal

In my opinion these are the best and also they last forever, which makes them well worth the money. However, they aren't easy to find these days. You will need bobby pins or heavy-duty open pins to hold them on your head.

Plastic

Cheaper, but they do the job. Some versions come with incorporated bristles designed to hold them on the head without grips. I hate these — they always seem to get caught in the hair. Choose plain ones like those in the photograph.

Velcro

Widely available in many sizes, they are easy to keep in position but not so easy to remove because of the little bristles that hold them to your head.

Foam

Cheap and cheerful, but they tend to get squashed if you wind the hair too tightly around them. Some types have an attachment which clips them securely. If not you can only use open pins to hold them.

Bendy curlers

These can be used for tight little curls and ringlets.

D.I.Y. rollers

You can make your own rollers from big sausages of cotton wool. This is what we did in the 1960s. It takes longer for the hair to dry but is great in an emergency.

Plastic rollers

Velcro rollers

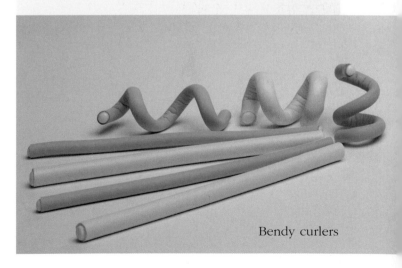

Bendy curlers

What size roller?

Well, basically the larger the roller, the looser the set will be. So if you want tight little 30s waves and curls you should choose small rollers. However, with a lot of 20th century styles, e.g. 1950s sets, several different sizes would be used; larger rollers on the top of the head, graduating to little ones at the nape of the neck.

Large

This size gives soft movement to mid-length hair and is the *only* size you can use for long hair. If you try to put smaller rollers in very long hair, it will take ages to dry and the weight of the hair will loosen the curl anyway.

Medium

The most useful of all the sizes. Depending on how you brush the set out, they give waves or curls which can also be backcombed into smooth fullness.

Small

Essential for tight little hairstyles. Hair set with these can be shaped into close waves or bubbly curls. Little rollers will hold shorter hair at the nape of the neck or in front of the ears securely.

Right: A selection of pins and clips *(see overleaf)*.

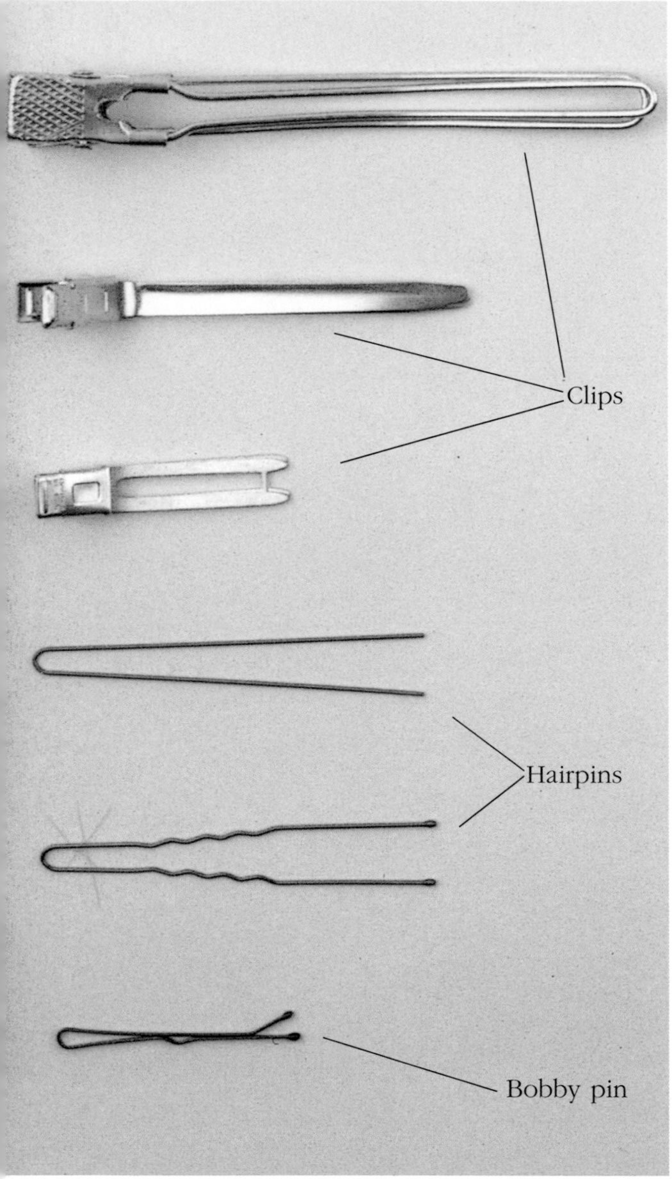

Clips

Metal clips are useful for both setting hair and holding it in place, for example, when you are working at the back of your head.

Large
These are normally used to hold hair in place as you style it (for example, they are useful for creating a French pleat — see page 36). There is nothing more frustrating than hair falling down as you are trying to put it up, but with long clips in place you have total control. Remove them *carefully* after spraying the hairstyle well.

Small
These are most useful for holding pincurls (see page 32) in position and replaced open pins for this purpose. Use either on wet or spray-gelled hair. Before rollers were invented these clips were used to set styles. They work well if you want to create a tight set or narrow waves across the back of the hair.

PIN TIP

❊ If you find that fine pins fall out of your hair, try bending them like this:

It is a little tricky taking them out afterwards but worth it!

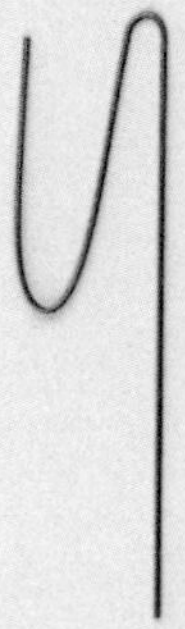

Pins

It is almost impossible to put hair up or create the elaborate styles of past centuries without these vital tools, so let's look at them carefully.

Bobby pins

What would we do without this great invention? These wonderful pins secure wigs and hairpieces, keep hair up and fulfil a multitude of other important tasks. There are two sizes:

Large
This size is most useful for holding long, heavy hair or head-dresses securely.

Small
Smaller bobby pins are excellent for all period styles, especially when used in conjunction with hairpins. Choose the color

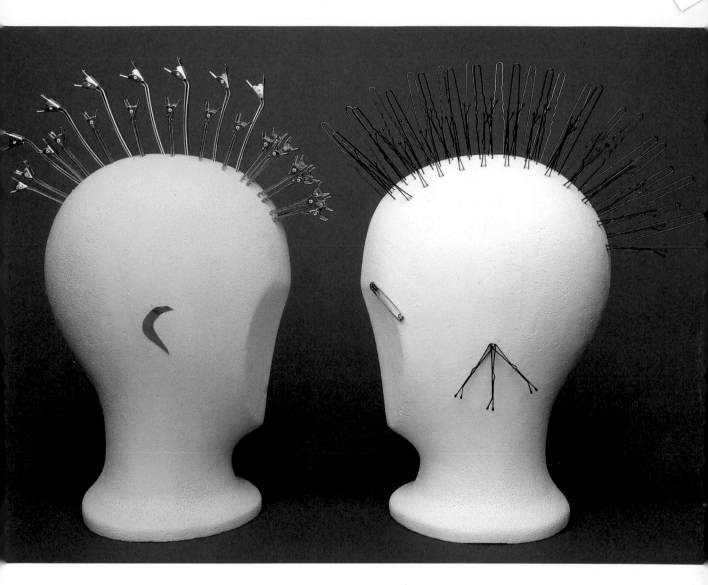

closest to your hair or wig and, if possible, buy mat pins which don't catch the light.

NOTE: You will need to open the pin before sliding it into your hair!

Hairpins

Hairpins have been in use since ancient times — originally they were made from bone and later from tortoiseshell. Nowadays they are usually metal and two lengths and weights are available. You *always* need to use them to put up your own hair or add a piece to it.

Heavy pins

Use these for maximum hold *after* you have secured the hair or wig with bobby pins. The longer ones work best if you are dealing with a lot of hair.

Fine pins

These are best for finishing styles or holding stray pieces of hair in place. They don't have the strength to hold heavy hair.

19

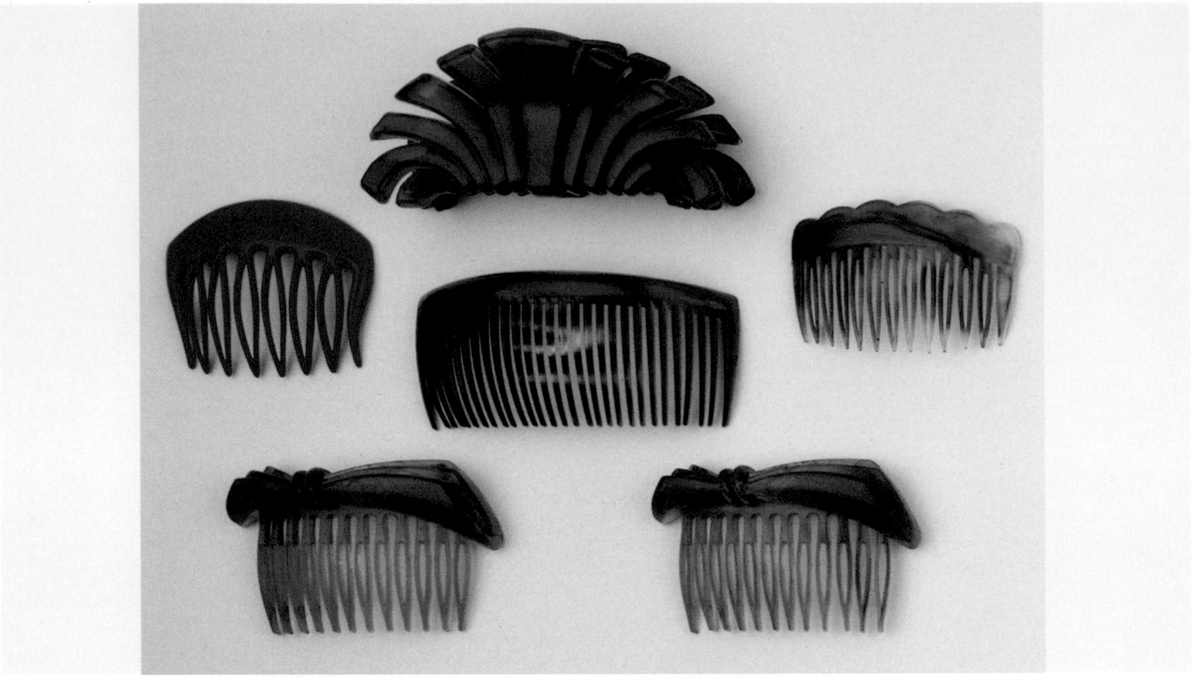

Decorative combs

Combs are very useful for a number of period styles. All Edwardian women used them and they were in common use right up to the 1960s. Brown ones are the most versatile.

> ***COMB TIP***
>
> ❊ Combs can fall out easily. See page 33 for instructions on how to put them in more securely.

Hairnets

There are many different types of hairnet, ranging from heavy mesh nets, usually in old-fashioned pastel shades, to fine mesh versions in hair colors. In Edwardian times, and later in the 1940s, heavy-duty nets called snoods were a fashion accessory worn at the back of the head. Wig nets do a different job — they keep your own hair secure under wigs.

Heavy mesh

These may remind you of your great granny but they are brilliant for keeping hair set with rollers or clips tidy while you hand dry it. If you don't use one, strands of hair will escape and spoil the set.

Fine mesh

This type of net can be used over your hair on stage to keep it in shape and will be invisible to the audience as long as you keep the elastic off your forehead. They are also useful if worn over a wig when you are taking it off because they prevent accidental damage to the style.

Bun nets

These small, fine nets are specifically made to cover chignons and buns and are really helpful in controlling wayward strands of hair. Secure the edge with fine hairpins.

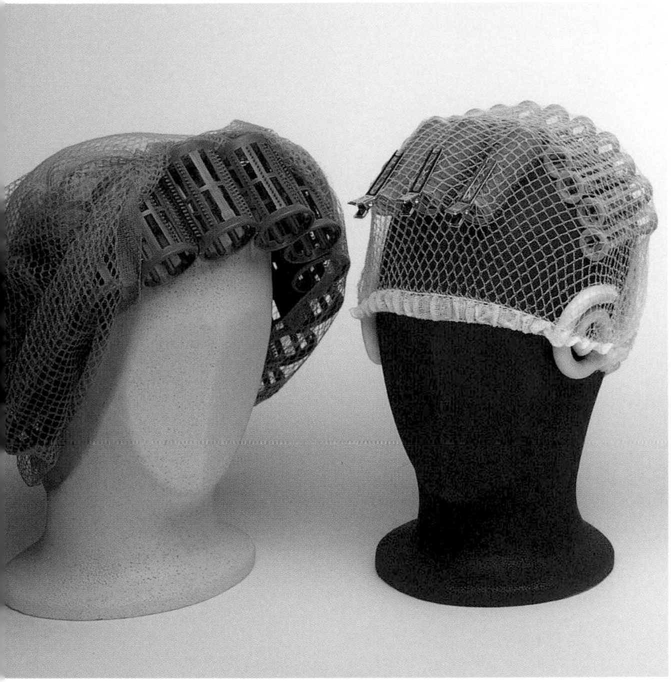

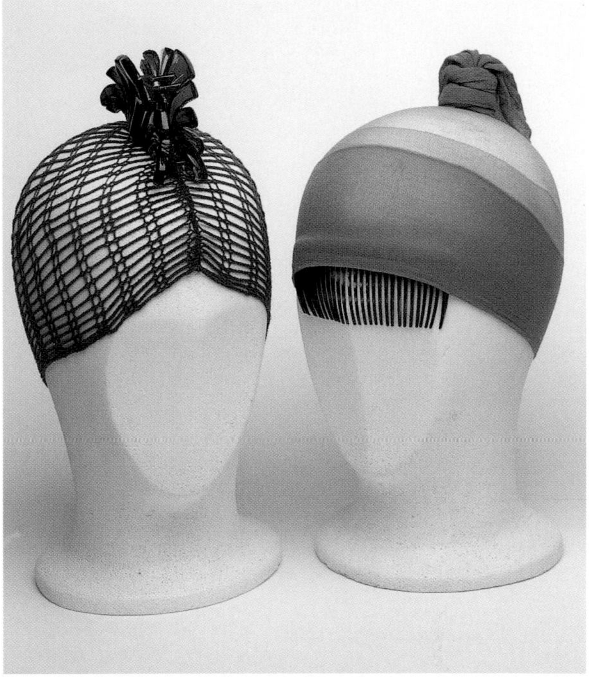

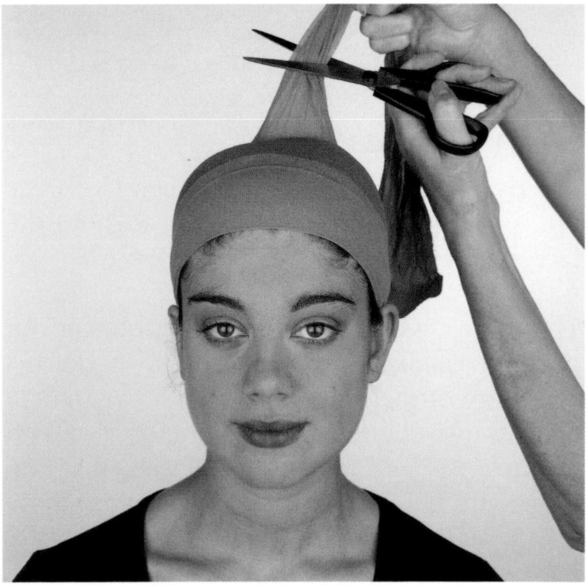

Wig nets

These are available from wig outlets and wig makers and are different from ordinary hair-nets. That type is too fragile to survive under a wig and will tear easily. Wig nets are tighter and stronger and prevent stray pieces of hair from escaping.

D.I.Y. nets

This is the professional actor's economy version — a stocking top. It's cheap, you get two for the price of one and it works just as well as the wig net. However, it has to be a traditional stocking rather than tights or hold-ups. Tights are no good because they have no welt at the top of the leg, and a hold-up would, I suspect, give you a nasty headache as well as being too thick on the welt. (See page 58 for instructions on how to make a D.I.Y. wig net.)

NET TIP

- Put both hands inside the net and carefully stretch it as you put it over your hair.

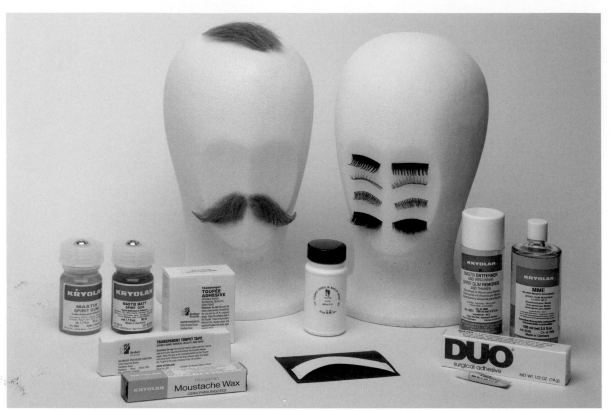

Spirit gum

If you are wearing a wig with a hair lace front you will need to use spirit gum to hold the lace securely to the sides of the face.

There are several types available, but for our purpose the mat is best because it doesn't show up under the lights. Men wearing a false moustache need spirit gum too, but over a run of shows can become sensitive to ordinary spirit gum (see page 71). I always advise using medicated spirit gum — Kryolan make a good one.

Duo adhesive

This is a latex adhesive which comes in a tube and is used extensively by people who wear prostheses in their daily lives. If you are sensitive to all spirit gums this is the answer — it is virtually impossible to be allergic to Duo adhesive. You can use it for false eyelashes too, although lashes do usually come with their own adhesive.

Spirit gum remover

You can remove gum with surgical spirit but a proper remover will be much kinder to your skin. There are several types available including an extra-mild version.

Toupee tape

This is like double-sided tape but is a special version made for wigs. Its main function is to secure toupees and the little slip-unders, worn by many top actors. You can buy it as half-inch strips, in a roll or in little moustache shapes.

Moustache wax

Soft wax for styling moustaches is sold in small tubes. You can buy clear or dark brown.

Wig blocks

If you are wearing a wig for a show it is important to keep it on a block (a head) between performances. You will find that it will keep its shape infinitely better if you do, and should you need to tidy up the wig you *must* do this on a block. Usually blocks come either as the rather grand hessian-covered ones used by wig-makers or the more humble polystyrene types which are more generally available. The latter is fine for our purpose. There are also collapsible ones around but these can cause problems, collapsing when you least expect it. If you are styling a wig on a block you will also need special wig pins to hold it to the block securely.

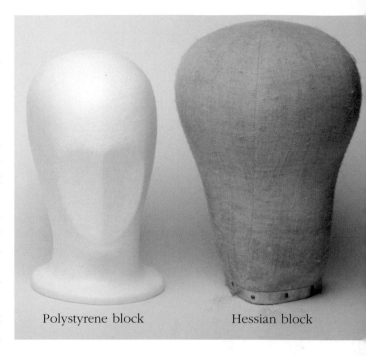

Polystyrene block   Hessian block

Wig clamp

Serious wig styling would require a clamp like this, which is fixed to the edge of the table. The wig block then fits onto the clamp securely and you can angle it to suit your purpose.

Wig spray

You can buy special spray for wigs but in my experience it sometimes clogs the hair so I prefer to use ordinary spray gel.

Hairspray or spray gel

It is absolutely vital to use this every time you style your hair and it is also helpful when wearing a wig. I prefer spray gel because I find it doesn't build up so much in the hair.

Pomades and gels for men

There are many different types available, ranging from the famous Brylcreem essential for 1940s styles, to fine gels and waxes that give a natural effect.

Curling tongs, hotbrushes and heated rollers

These are useful when you are in a hurry, but they do dry your hair out if you use them consistently over a run of shows.

Section One

Using Your Own Hair

Using your own hair

With today's casual "wash and go" hairstyles, I have discovered that many people have never really learned how to handle and set their own hair for anything except the most basic styles, so this section is about working with your own hair for productions.

At first you may find that setting and styling hair can be quite daunting if you don't normally do it in your everyday life. So here you will discover how to design the style you need, whether to use rollers or hairclips to achieve the movement and shape of the hair, and how to use them properly. Among the many other things covered, I have included a comprehensive guide to putting up long hair securely because there are few things more disturbing than to feel your hair falling down when you are acting. Since many actresses do not have hair that is long enough to put up successfully in period styles, there is also advice on attaching chignons and various other false pieces to give the illusion of more length.

There is also styling advice specifically for men, including tips for improving beards and moustaches, and sneaky ways of improving a weedy moustache. The section on hair products (see page 45) offers suggestions on hair coloring, which I know men will find particularly useful. With the big range of permanent or semi-permanent products available it is helpful to know what to choose.

Designing the pli for a hairstyle

What is a pli? Well, basically it is a professional term that is used to describe the setting pattern for a hairstyle. Of course today's more casual blow-dried styles don't have sets — they rely on good cutting — but as soon as you use rollers or clips in your hair it is enormously helpful to understand about the pli. When we look back over the 20th century we can see that for most of the first sixty years, and certainly from the 1920s to the 1960s, fashionable women had their hair set and dried. So if you need to style your hair like Jean Harlow, create Rita Hayworth's wonderful 1940s waves, or recreate Marilyn Monroe's famous 50s style, sorting out the size of rollers you need and where to position them is really useful.

The basic thing that you need to understand when setting hair properly, is that the angle of the rollers or clips will dictate the direction of the hair when it is brushed out. Get this wrong and you will be disappointed in the final result.

Let's take an example. Supposing you want your hair to be set back off the face with soft curls behind your ears and across the back of your head. Well, first of all you will need to choose the right size rollers. For this you would need medium-sized and smaller ones (but not too small). The rollers would be positioned across the head with the hair rolled around them from the front. The medium-sized rollers would be at the front and on the top of the head, with the smaller ones at the back to give a tighter curl. If this sounds complicated, the diagrams that follow should

help. Sometimes a style can be achieved with rollers alone, sometimes you need a combination of rollers and clips, and sometimes it will only be achievable with clips.

You will need to use a setting lotion, gel or mousse and also a tail comb to section and roll the hair. If you run out of setting gel, beer is a brilliant substitute. It gives a really firm set and the smell disappears in the drying. When the hair is set, always cover it with a hairnet before drying it.

SET TIP

✳ If you have never put a roller or a clip in your hair before this, turn to pages 30-32 to learn the correct way to use them before you attempt setting.

Roller pli front

1930s front

1950s front

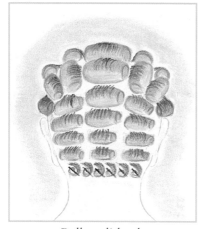

Roller pli back

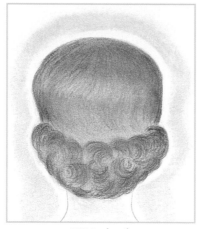

1930s back

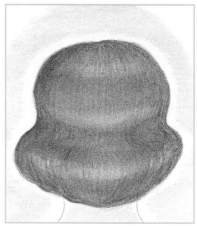

1950s back

These two plis give you some idea of the way to set hair. Remember, the neater the sections, the better the result. Also, the angle of the rollers will determine the movement of the finished hairstyle so that if, for example, you want your hair to come forward onto your face, you roll it from behind the rollers. Once you have mastered that principle you can create any style you need.

Roller pli

Here is a basic roller pli for medium length hair. The hair is sectioned and set with large rollers on the top, graduating to medium and then small as you go down the head. Where the hair is too short or there is no room for a roller, pincurls are used. At the front the hair in the middle section is rolled back from the face, but the rest is rolled to the sides. At the back the hair is all rolled downwards.

This is a versatile pli which works well for several styles including the 1930s and 1950s sets shown here. It can also be brushed out to give fullness to a glamorous modern style.

1930s soft set

This typical 1930s style has two keynote 30s features – a waved front and curls. The front is backcombed and taken to one side in a big wave and the lower hair is brushed into curls.

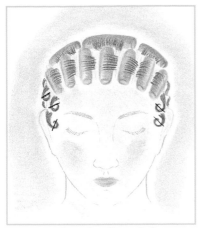

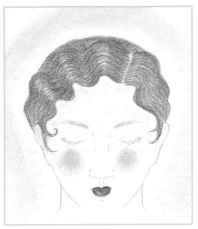

Pincurl and roller pli front

1920s front

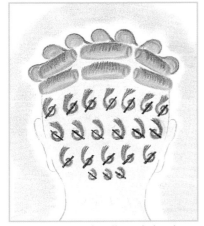

Pincurl and roller pli back

1920s back

Clips across the waves

To keep the smoother hair in place as you do the curls, secure it horizontally with large clips, then spray the style and remove them.

1950s style
Here the pli creates a typical 50s hairstyle with the top backcombed and brushed carefully back. The lower hair is turned under (brush it over your hand to get the shape) and there is top backcombing for fullness.

Pincurl and roller pli

This is a pli for a waved hairstyle on short hair of the type extensively worn in the 1920s and early 30s. Originally the whole head would have been done with pincurls, but the combination of small rollers and pincurls shown in the diagram is easier to do. The front is set in a side parting with the rollers going across the head instead of back.

The hair is rolled to the left on one side of the parting and to the right on the other. There are two rows of small rollers at the back and then rows of pincurls. These alternate from left to right as they go down the head to create waves. The style is then brushed out into tight waves. As you do this you can clip across the rows to keep them in position (see photo above). When you have finished spray it with spray gel and remove them.

Rollers ~

how to use them

Rollers give hairstyles volume and are best used for medium to long hair to give a soft set or movement. They are easy to use but many people use them incorrectly. If you just grab hanks of hair at random and roll them up you will find that there are always strands in the wrong place. Before you begin rolling the hair, you need to work out a pattern for the rollers in order to achieve the style you require (see page 27) or the result will be unsatisfactory.

Here is how to achieve the perfect result:

1. Using a tail comb, section the hair into a rectangle approximately the same size as your roller. Make sure that your partings are very clean with no stray bits of hair out of place.

2. Comb the hair through, stretching it gently away from your head and clasp it firmly between two fingers. Place the roller behind the sectioned hair if it is to be styled back from your face, or in front if it is going forward, and move it up the hair until you are quite close to the ends.

3. Comb the ends over the roller and with the tail of your comb tuck them under it. Then carefully roll the roller down to your scalp tucking in any stray hairs as you go.

4. Finally, secure the roller to your head with a heavy-duty pin, or with two bobby pins pushed through either end of it.

NOTE: You work in exactly the same way with bendy curlers except that you bend the ends over when you finish.

ROLLER TIP

❊ If your hair slips as you do this, wrap a piece of tissue around the ends before you start rolling.

Pincurls ~

how to achieve the perfect curl

If you want a really tight-looking hairstyle, say for a 1920s or 30s production, or you need little curls around your hairline, then pincurls are the answer. This was a popular method of curling hair before the Perm was invented.

Just as with rollers, you will need to section the hair carefully before you begin, only this time you make a square and not a rectangle. The more perfect your square, the better the end result.

1. Using a tail comb, make a little square section of hair. It mustn't be too big or the curl will be difficult to dry properly.

2. Comb through the hair and starting from the root end, carefully wrap it round one finger.

3. Gently slide the hair down to the end of your finger until it comes off the end. Tuck the hair end into the center and lay the curl flat against your head making sure that you stay within the section. Secure it with a metal clip across the center (**a**), or two crossed bobby pins (**b**).

1
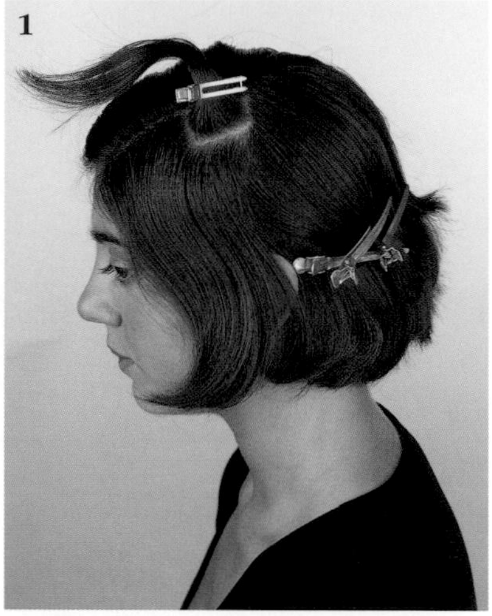

2
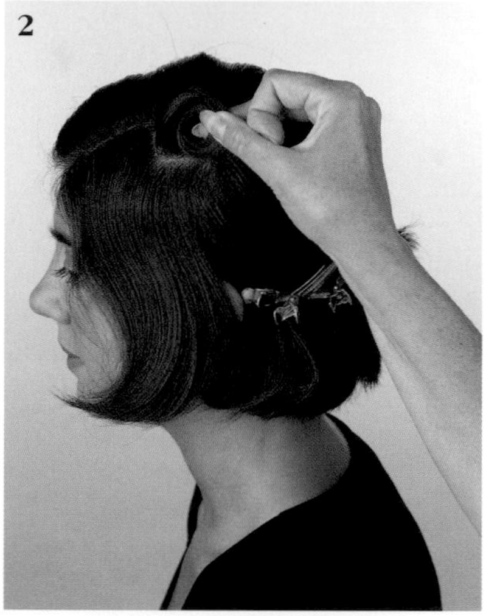

CURL TIP

- As you lay the curl flat to your head, be careful not to twist the roots of the hair or you will get a kinked effect.
- You can use a little piece of tissue wrapped around the hair to stop it slipping as you work. This is especially helpful with tiny curls.

3a
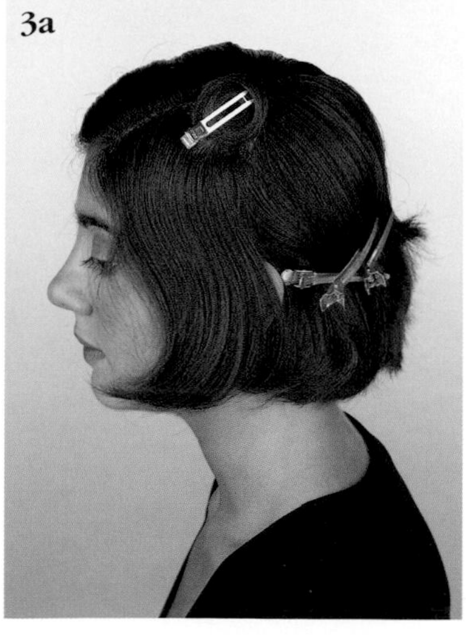

3b
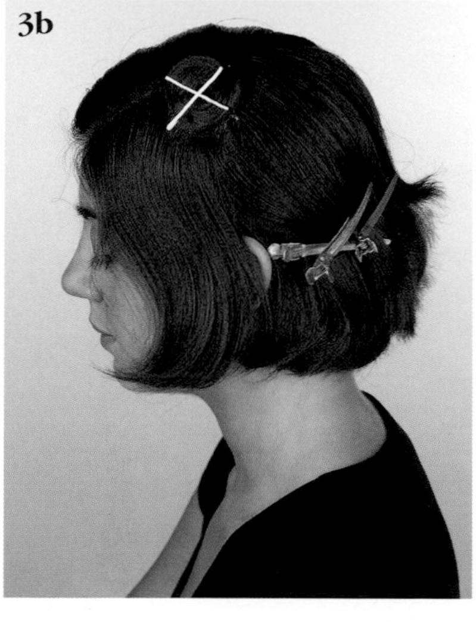

Using a decorative comb

These combs can easily fall out of your hair, particularly if it is freshly washed. When they were widely used in the past it was rare for women to wash their hair more than once a week, and the combs were held in more securely as a result. Follow the instructions by the photographs to put them in safely.

1. Place comb in hair the wrong way round and with the curved side flat to the head.

2. Turn the comb and push firmly forward into desired position.

3. Here is the comb securely in place.

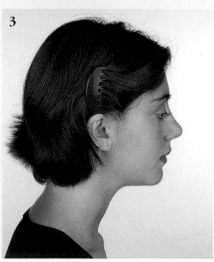

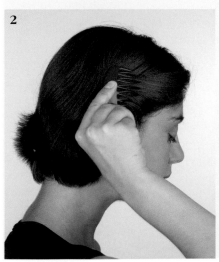

33

Backcombing or teasing hair

Many hairstyles need height and volume. People with thick hair have this built in; the rest of us are not so lucky. This is where backcombing can be very useful. It is a technique that has, I suspect, been around for a long time. It is, for example, impossible to achieve a splendid 1960s beehive hairdo without it.

Interestingly, girls in those days would often backcomb their hair at the beginning of the week, take the pins out at night but leave the backcombing in their hair to re-pin the next morning — it saved time.

There is a wrong and a right way to backcomb. With the first way you get minimal volume, but with the second you can achieve spectacular results. Here is how you do it properly.

You need:

- a tail comb
- a brush
- metal clips

To achieve really good results you need to work in sections starting from the front of your hair.

Take the front section (it shouldn't be too wide), comb it up from your head and clasp it tightly between two fingers (it should feel stretched). Then take the comb behind the hair at the roots with the teeth pointing forwards and, working upwards towards the ends, comb in little strokes to force some of the hair back down. You must hold the ends tightly as you do this.

You will find that if you do this properly the section of hair stands up on its own. Lift that section forward and take another one behind it and repeat the process. Keep going across the head until you have reached the back. Then do the sides, starting at the ears.

Once you have finished backcombing, lightly brush the top hair into the required shape.

NOTE: Sometimes only the front hair will need backcombing.

BACKCOMBING TIPS

❋ You cannot backcomb greasy hair — it won't work.

❋ When you are brushing the backcombing out, hold the roots flat to your head with your other hand to prevent pulling the hair.

Creating a French pleat

This has to be one of the most useful techniques for any actress to learn. A French pleat down the back of your head gives a really secure base to which you can pin most hairpieces including chignons, curls, ringlets and falls. There really is no better way to style your hair for this purpose.

French pleats are also an integral part of the elegant upswept hairstyles of the 1950s and 60s. Think of Audrey Hepburn in *Breakfast at Tiffany's* or Grace Kelly at her fairytale Monaco wedding. Neither of their hairstyles would have worked without French pleats.

To make a perfect pleat you will need:

- a tail comb

- a hairbrush

- bobby pins and hairpins

- metal clips

- hairspray or spray gel

1. You begin by backcombing the hair (see page 34 if you don't know how to do this) to give it more body and make it easier to handle.

2. Section off the front of your hair and take it forward out of your way. Now carefully brush one side of your hair back and upwards (clip it in front of your ear if it looks like it may fall out of place). Then, holding it in place under one hand, run bobby pins down the center of the back of your head as in the picture. Spray well.

3. Put your hand up over the bobby pins and brush the rest of the hair across your hand. Remove your hand and fold the hair under into a vertical roll. Use hairpins to pin it along the folded edge, catching them under the bobby pins to secure them. You will need big hairpins initially and then finer ones to tidy the edge of the roll. Spray well.

4. Brush the front hair back and if necessary hold in place with fine hairpins. Spray and remove clips *carefully*. If the front looks a little flat take the end of the tail comb under it and gently lift the hair.

Rats

PLEAT TIP

❋ Hair goes up more easily if it isn't freshly washed and soft.

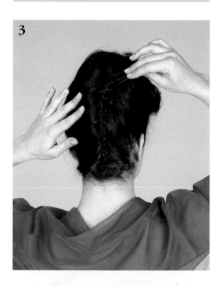

3

4

Those towering, powdered hairstyles of the Restoration period were stuffed with rats — at that time made of prickly horsehair. Gibson Girls wore them as a base for their smooth elegant coiffures and the elaborate rolled hair of the 1940s was achieved with their support. In our world of 'wash and go' hairstyling, rats are little used, BUT for theatre and film they are invaluable in helping to create the styles of the past. Nearly every woman will be familiar with one type of rat — the bun ring, a simple way of controlling longer hair and making a neat shape at the nape of the neck. Your great, great granny

Ready-made rats

almost certainly used one at one time or another and they are still available in big stores. But there are other shapes, generally sausage-like, which wig stockists sell. You can also make your own, which is much cheaper and just as effective and has the advantage in that you can make any length that you wish.

NOTE: Rats only work with medium-length or long hair.

Making a rat

You will need:

• a piece of stocking

• crêpe wool (available from theatrical stockists and fancy dress stores)

• needle and thread, pins

Method 1

1. Cut the stocking to the length that you need and lay it flat on the table.

2. Unravel the crêpe wool and bunch it into the shape that you need.

3. Lay the wool along the center of the stocking leaving an empty area at each end.

4. Fold the stocking round the wool and pin before stitching the folds and ends — you should finish up with a little fat sausage like the one in the picture.

Method 2

1. Cut the stocking and machine it into a tube shape. Trim away any excess.

2. Turn it inside out and stuff with crêpe wool.

3. Stitch the ends.

Bun ring

Use Method 2 and stuff one end inside the other. Turn remaining edge over and stitch.

How to use your rat

Here are three styles that you can create using rats. I suggest that you read right through the instructions first before you begin.

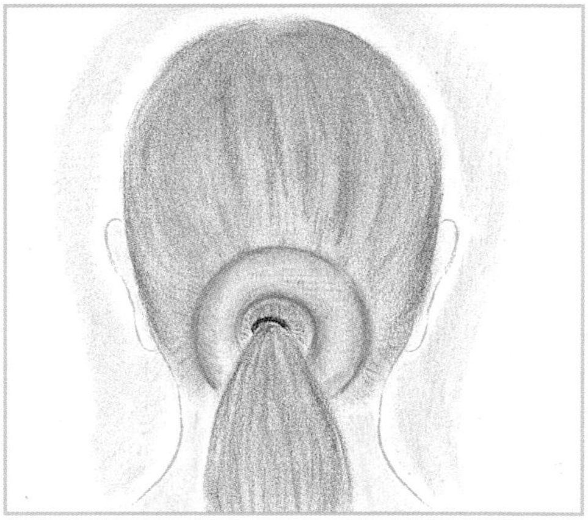

A bun ring in place. The position would vary according to period.

Making a bun

You will need:

- a bun ring
- tail comb and brush
- hairpins
- a covered elastic band
- hairspray
- a bun net (optional)

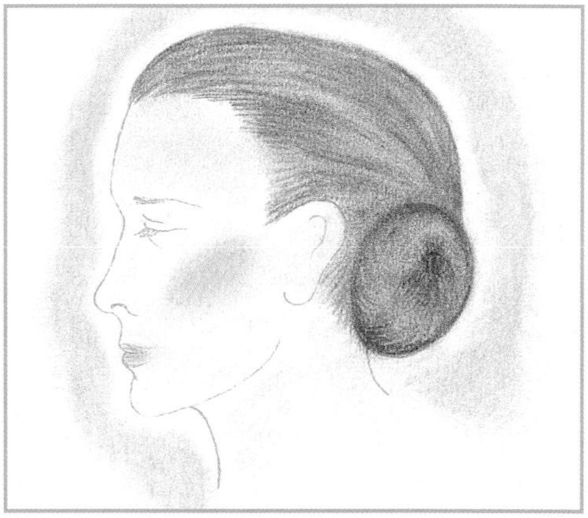

The finished effect

Brush your hair back smoothly and secure it with the covered elastic band. I would now spray the smoothed hair with hairspray — you don't want strands falling while you are working on the back of your head. Tease or backcomb the loose hair to give it more volume and make it easier to control, then pull it through the ring tightly. The next bit is tricky because you can't see what you are doing — you have to feel it. Spread the hair around the ring and brush it lightly, then, making sure the ring is tight to your head, tuck the hair in behind it all round (a tail comb is helpful here) and pin the bun to your smoothed hair with hairpins. Spray well. Check in mirror.

> ***BUN TIPS***
>
> ❊ If this is quite a large bun or you have heavy hair, you may need to use bobby pins for more security.
>
> ❊ If little pieces of hair stick out from the center, solve this problem with a bun net. I think it is always a good idea to use one anyway.

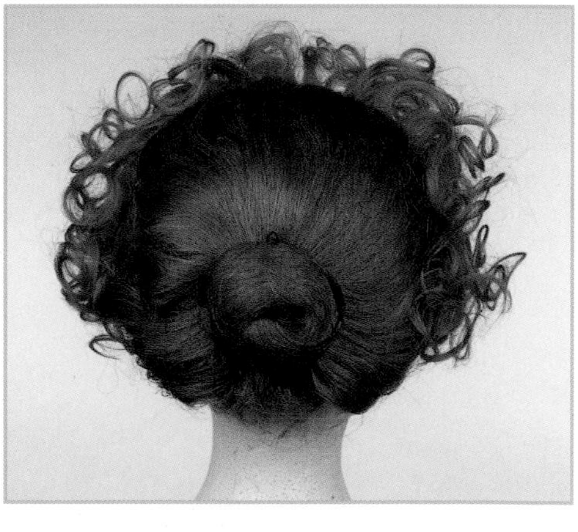

Edwardian Gibson Girl style

You will need:

• 2 long rats (measure the distance between your ears back and front — you will need rats that are a bit shorter than that)

• a tail comb and brush

• bobby pins, long and short hairpins

• a covered elastic band

• metal clips (for holding the hair while you work)

• hairspray

Position of rats

Unless it is very thick, it helps to tease or backcomb *all* your hair before you start. Then brush the front section forward and clip it out of your way. Brush the rest down at the back and pin a rat across it in a curved shape, using bobby pins at the ends. The pins should be behind your ears. Loosen the front hair, making sure that it is smoothly forward, and pin the other rat across the top of your head, again placing bobby pins at the ends. Check in the mirror to ensure that the back one isn't too low and the front one isn't too far forward. Now comes the tricky bit — you need to gather all the hair in one hand, smoothing it over the rats all round, and catch the end length in the elastic band. Sometimes, if the hair is not so long, it is

The finished effect

A wig version
of the style

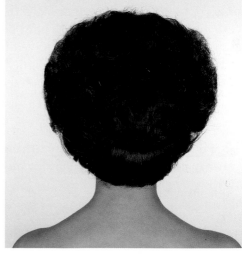

easier to do the two sections separately. Spray the first one, secure it with metal clips and then do the other. If you have pulled the hair too tightly and squashed your rats, use the end of the comb to loosen it.

Make an attractive shape with the ends of the hair, pin it and then spray the whole head well. You can tease out little curls in front of your ears if you wish.

1940s rolled hairstyle

Here is a simple way of using a rat to recreate a typical style of the period on shoulder length hair.

You will need:

- rollers or heated tongs
- one long sausage-shaped rat
- hairspray or gel
- short fine hairpins and bobby pins
- tail comb and hairbrush

Begin by styling the front hair. An easy way is to make a side parting and either set each side on rollers or curl it with heated tongs to create soft waves curving backwards on each side of the face. Pin the rest of the hair back behind your ears and spray the front.

Backcomb the rest to make it easier to roll and smooth the top layer. Now run a curved row of bobby pins across your back hair in line with your ear tips. Pin the rat across your head in a low curve from ear to ear, securing it behind them.

Carefully roll the length of your hair up over the rat, tucking the hair in firmly behind it using your fingers and the end of the tail comb. (You may need to brush it lightly at this point.) When you have tucked it all in, pin the edge of the roll to the rest of your hair with the fine hairpins, catching them behind the row of bobby pins to keep it in place. Adjust the rolled hair behind your ears to hide the rat ends. Spray well and then give your head a little shake to make sure the roll feels secure. Add more pins as necessary.

GIBSON GIRL STYLE TIPS

❋ Never do this with freshly washed hair — it will slip all over the place!

❋ Using a tail comb to lift the hair once it's up adjusts the shape to suit your face.

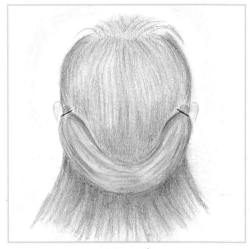

Position of rat

The finished effect

Using your own hair ~ men

Since actors generally use their own hair in productions it is worth considering the advantage of different lengths.

Very short hair

Clearly there is little you can do to change a hairstyle like this which, of course, can be limiting. However, the advantage of it is that it throws the emphasis onto the face. The disadvantage is that you will find yourself wearing wigs in many period productions ('period' can be taken to mean any time prior to the 1980s).

Short hair with some length on top

This length is surprisingly versatile and can easily be styled in many ways. It is particularly suitable for period styles ranging from Victorian to modern.

Just below the ears

Hair this length, especially if it has some curl in it or is wavy, works well for Elizabethan dandies, 19th century gentlemen and the 1960s and 70s.

Long hair

In many ways this can be as limiting as very short hair. It only suits some periods. However, it comes into its own for Jacobean tragedies, Restoration comedies and the musical *Hair*.

Trendy cuts

Many sharp fashion cuts are extremely difficult to restyle for productions. I am thinking particularly of hairstyles that are long on the crown and very short at the back. If you are an actor, it's best to avoid these.

A simple way to create the illusion of more hair

It is a fact of life that many men have naturally thin hair, and actors are no exception. Many will inevitably suffer some hair loss by their middle years. So what is to be done to solve the problem when acting?

Some actors resort to hair weaves and implants, others to toupees, but when we are talking about small areas of loss or a thinning of short hair all that is really needed is something to give the illusion of thicker hair when you are performing.

There are a number of hair thickening shampoos and conditioners on the market and also products like Mane which coat the hair follicles giving a thicker effect. But an alternative method, ideal for the stage, is to use cake make-up, which is very effective in creating the illusion of more hair or hiding a bald patch.

Cake make-up is a theatrical foundation which comes in various shades of brown, brownish-black and black. It is water-based, making it easy to wash out, and is ideal for hiding small bald patches, thickening up short sparse hair and giving the illusion of thickness to beards, moustaches and side whiskers that haven't quite made it. It is produced by Bob Kelly and Kryolan, and is available in most theatrical stores. Cake eyeliner is a mini version of the same product.

NOTE: Cake make-up is easily removed with soap and water.

Hiding a bald patch or thickening very short hair

For this you will need a cake make-up to match your natural hair color and a small open-textured cosmetic sponge.

Damp the sponge with water and work some cake make-up onto it (not too much or it will look heavy on the skin). Before you begin to apply the make-up to your scalp, try a little on the back of your hand to see if you have the right degree of color on the sponge. Then stipple the cake make-up carefully over the area that you wish to color. To bulk up thin and very short hair you need to work the color over the whole head as I am doing in the photograph.

NOTE: This technique only works for small patches of baldness.

Filling in a beard, moustache or side whiskers

For this you will need cake make-up in the correct color and a fine brush. Wet the brush a little and stroke some color onto it. Then paint little hairs among the real ones, taking care to draw them in at the same angle as the natural hair.

Darkening fair, ginger or gray facial hair

Cake make-up and cake mascara are useful for an actor whose natural facial hair is either too fair to show up on stage or is the wrong color. They are also invaluable if you are given a false moustache that is the wrong color. To change the color or darken your own hair, you will need the appropriate color in either of these products and a small toothbrush. Wet the brush a little, rub it over the make-up and apply to the hair, working across the growth. This way you prevent the make-up from going onto your skin (it is very difficult to remove blobs of dark make-up from under facial hair).

One or two days' beard stubble

Cake make-up gives a very realistic beard stubble. It is easy to apply and easy to remove if you have to become clean-shaven quickly. You can buy special little square stipple sponges to do this but I prefer an open-textured sponge myself. With the square ones there is a danger of ending up with a lot of dirty-looking squares around your chin if you are not careful.

To create the stubble, damp a small area of the sponge and take up a little cake make-up (dab some onto the back of your hand to check if it is too wet — if so, squeeze the sponge out). Then gently stipple the color onto the areas that you shave. Be sure to go under your chin as well and check that there are no straight edges to the stubble.

BEARD STUBBLE TIP

❋ To remove this quickly you can use cake make-up in a skin tone. Have this ready on a sponge by the stage (ideally with a mirror). Just wipe the skin tone firmly over the stubble to blend it away.

Hair products

Going into a drugstore with its shelf upon shelf of coloring and styling products can be a daunting experience. I know from talking to actors that when they have to color their hair for a part, panic can set in — what should they use? And just how do you decide which kind of styling product is right for you? Of course you could simplify the matter and go to a hairdresser but not every actor can afford that. So here is a simple guide to some of the products you will come across.

Shampoo

Let's start with shampoo. Basically you choose a product according to your hair type. The bottle will always tell you if it is for dry, greasy, or that illusive thing, normal hair. However, manufacturers like to sell us lots of products and this is where it becomes complicated. There are shampoos for damaged hair, lifeless hair, bleached hair, colored hair, sunburned hair — you name it there is a shampoo for it. I expect one for sensitive hair to appear on the market at any moment. But all that you really need is a good quality gentle shampoo which won't strip the natural oil (sebum) from the hair, particularly if you wash it frequently. Beware of using a strong shampoo on greasy hair because this will accelerate the natural oil production and make the hair greasier.

Conditioners

I am always doubtful about "all in one" shampoos and conditioners; it puts me in mind of cleansers with moisturizers in them. If your hair needs a conditioner it is better to buy a separate product.

Hair dressings

This market has grown enormously in the last few years, encouraged by new styles generated by club culture. Apart from the ever-popular gels, you can also find waxes, putties and even a product called Hair Liquorice. Read the label and see if it will do the job you require. For example, to create a glossy 1950s style of the type worn by Elvis Presley, you will need to use a shiny hair dressing like Brylcreem. For 1920s male styles, the hair will need a product that will keep it smooth to the head. One universally useful hair dressing, which I mention frequently in this book, is firm-hold spray gel. This product is extremely good for controlling wayward hair.

Hair thickeners

There are products available which put a coating on the hair shafts to give the hair a thicker appearance (we show one called Mane on page 47). They come in a limited range of colors, and there are also colorless versions. Sometimes men with thinning hair will find these helpful, but don't expect a miracle if your hair is really thin. There are also thickening shampoos and conditioners on the market, and waxes that claim to do the same thing. These may also be worth trying.

Hair colorants

The hair product companies wisely treat us all as complete beginners and give very precise instructions with their products. Some even include polythene gloves to protect our hands. *Always* read the instructions carefully and if unsure consult a friend who has experience of using this type of product.

There are two types of colorants available — permanent and semi-permanent.

Permanent colors

You will need to remember that a product labeled 'permanent' on the box is not necessarily going to last for months and months. Because your hair is a living thing it grows and falls out constantly. This means that, depending on the speed that your hair grows, the roots will show through in your natural color somewhere between six weeks to a couple of months after the tint. Then you will have to retouch the color. It is best if you only do this to the roots to avoid damage to hair that has already been colored.

Semi-permanent colors

There are a variety of semi-permanent coloring products available, ranging from colored shampoos and mousses, to tints that last up to twenty-four shampoos. When you browse through these products you will notice that the time the color will last is always quoted on the packaging. Most semi-permanents will not last very long if you shampoo daily, and in this case you would be wise to have permanent color on your hair. Here is a rough guide to what is available at present:

Color Shampoos

These generally last until the next hair wash. Helpful for keeping permanent colors (which gradually fade in intensity) bright.

Color Mousses

Used after shampooing to add color, some last only a couple of hair washes, others claim to stay in for up to five.

WARNING

With both permanent and semi-permanent colors there are some important rules to be aware of.

✻ Bleached hair — bleaching changes the structure of the hair shaft making it more porous. This means that if you use tints on bleached hair you could have a nasty surprise with the resulting color. Never use tints on bleached hair without professional advice.

✻ Hennaed hair — if your hair is hennaed you cannot guarantee that the tint color will be as you expected. Hennaed hair when tinted will either be more golden or have a copper tone.

Tints

These range from those that last 6-8 shampoos to others that stay in for up to 24 shampoos.

Lightening your hair

There is a new generation of permanent hair dyes called "high lift tints" which will lighten hair that isn't very dark. The resulting hair color will be four or five shades lighter than your natural color.

However, for a really blond effect, or if you have dark hair, you will need to use a bleach. You can do this yourself but please read the instructions carefully before you start because peroxide, which is the main ingredient in all bleaches, can damage your hair if you don't. Over-bleached hair can actually break off at the roots.

Spray-on color

The theatrical make-up companies sell temporary spray colors which range from black to bright perky colors. They are easy to use and just wash out after a performance. When using them, protect your clothes and the surrounding area and hold the can a short distance from your head, or you will get the color onto your scalp making it very difficult to remove. You will need help with spraying the back of your hair. Hair roots around the hairline, side whiskers, beards, eyebrows and moustaches can be done by spraying some color into a saucer and then applying it with a toothbrush.

Hiding gray hair

There are lots of products sold to women for covering gray hair and in general I feel that they work better than the ones made specifically for men. It is worth remembering that gray hair at the temples can be particularly resistant to these products. If you are wanting to hide just a little grayness, which usually first appears around the hairline area, see page 43 which discusses how cake make-up and mascara can provide a simple solution to the problem.

Graying hair

On occasion actors do terrible things to their hair to simulate grayness. White shoe dressing and powder are still, surprisingly, often used. Of course, they are cheap but they are not particularly convincing. The shoe polish gives a flat dead effect and powder, which looks as bad, can rise in a little cloud of dust when you touch it or remove a hat. In fact a silver hairspray gives by far the best effect. There are various grays on the market but the silver gives the hair more life and shine.

For small areas, such as side whiskers or gray at the temples, I use Kryolan Paintstick 1W. (This is a stick foundation in a very pale color.) You just take a little on your finger and lightly touch it over the hair you need to gray. The effect is of some gray hairs among the darker ones, which looks very natural. This also works well on eyebrows, moustaches and beards. Alternatively, you can buy hair mascaras for this purpose but I still prefer my own method.

Section Two

Wigs &
False Hair

False hair

False hair in one form or another is commonplace in film, television and theatre. It might be Queen Victoria's severe hairstyle, Adolf Hitler's moustache, Abraham Lincoln's beard or the golden curls of the chorus girls in the musical *Crazy For You* — they all involve false hair. Actors use it, wardrobe departments clean it and make-up designers like me work with it — it's everywhere. The term "false hair" can cover anything from an elaborate, towering Restoration wig, like the one pictured on the cover (actually two wigs put together), to a simple crêpe hair eyebrow or moustache. Even false eyelashes are false hair.

Since few actresses today have the long, luxurious tresses prized in past centuries as a woman's crowning glory, they will need the help of wigs and hairpieces for period plays. Similarly, not all actors have the time, or indeed the inclination, to grow or style a beard or moustache for a character, so a false one is the only alternative. Sometimes a production budget simply can't stretch to the hire of professional wigs and, as has happened to me in the past, you are expected to achieve miracles with a cheap synthetic fashion wig. Working with false hair can be daunting. How do you deal with the hair lace at the front of the wig? What is the solution if your moustache keeps falling off? If you have long hair and a short wig what do you do? In this section you will find all the information you require for working happily and confidently with false hair.

Attaching a false hairpiece

There are a variety of false pieces that you can attach to your own hair. They are generally used to create the illusion of fuller or longer hair for a character.

You can find some in department stores. Sometimes these synthetic pieces come as half heads of hair attached to Alice bands, sometimes as clusters of curls which clamp to the back of your head. You can also find pony tails and switches but most of the professional hairpieces available are made of real hair and are woven onto a mesh base. Ringlets are slightly different, coming often in rows on a tape, and may be synthetic. The real hairpieces often have a small comb sewn onto the edge to help attach them to your hair.

Before putting on a piece, you must either put your own hair into a French pleat (see page 36) or, if it is too short to do that, comb it back and secure it with bobby pins.

In either case be sure to spray your own hair well with hairspray to hold it in place. You will also need plenty of bobby pins and hairpins when you use a hairpiece.

Using a piece with an attached comb

I have deliberately used a darker color than the model's own hair so you can see which is real and which is false.

Put your hair into a French pleat or, if it is too short, secure it back from your face with bobby pins. Spray well. If you can't use a French pleat you must make a large pincurl at the back of your head for the comb to go into. If you don't do this the piece will gradually slip down your head.

Holding the piece, lift the little comb away from the base and gently push the teeth into the top of the French pleat or the pincurl as I am doing in the picture. This can be a bit fiddly if the teeth are quite close together.

Adjust the piece to your head, pressing it against your own hair and pin it all around the base until it feels really safe (shake your head to test this).

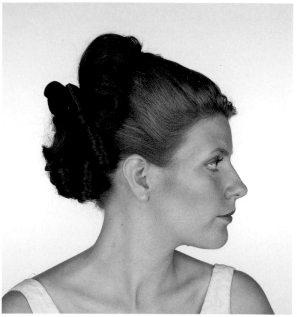

Finally, use fine pins to blend the false hair into your own. If the pins keep slipping out, see the pin tip on page 18.

I have used the same false piece in a different way on the opposite page.

Adding a false chignon

A chignon is usually worn in a fairly low position at the back of the head. This means that a French pleat would need to be folded in a lower position than normal. To achieve this, comb your hair downwards rather than up and fold and pin it (the resulting pleat will be shorter than usual). Attach the chignon in the same way as previously described, but making sure that the pleat doesn't show above the chignon.

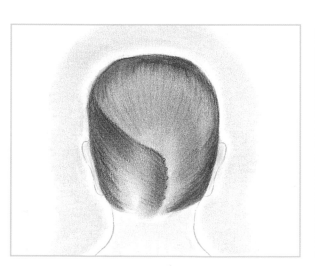

Low French pleat

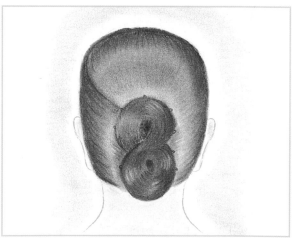

Chignon in place

Attaching ringlets

These are often bought ready-made in rows on a tape. Usually you cut off the number that you require and make a bunch for each side of the head. You may need them in front, over or behind your ears. Either way you will need to section off the front hair and take it forward before attaching the ringlets. Once they are firmly pinned into place you can take the front hair back to hide the base of the ringlets. Occasionally ringlets are worn right around the back of the head, in which case you will need enough hair to cover the tape there, although often ribbons or flowers can be used to help hide it.

Ringlets position – edge hidden by natural hair

HAIR LACE TIPS

✳ Always make your face up before the wig goes on. If make-up gets on the lace it makes it more noticeable.

✳ Some older hair lace wigs have rather frilly edges. A few little dabs of spirit gum across the forehead under the lace should solve that problem; use a dryish sponge to press the lace down.

✳ Hair lace wigs should be cleaned by a pro- fessional wig person.

WARNING

✳ Never cut the hair lace back without the wig department's permission — you could ruin the wig.

Hair lace wigs & toupees

These are the crème de la crème of the wig world. They are usually made from real hair and hand-knotted, which of course makes them expensive to buy. Hair lace wigs are always used when an actor requires a style that brushes back from the forehead — the less expensive synthetic wigs have too obvious a hairline edge to look realistic. Hair lace wigs have a fine skin-colored net at the front which stretches across the forehead and down in front of the ears. The finer this net is, the more expensive the wig will be. When the net is stretched and glued down it becomes invisible and the hairline looks natural.

The same techniques can be applied to toupees, and generations of top actors, movie stars and pop idols have benefited from these. A toupee is a small front piece or half-wig which gives the illusion of plenty of hair.

How to put on a hair lace wig

There are a few things that you will need to bear in mind when you wear a hair lace wig. The most important one is that this type of wig needs careful handling. If you are careless you can easily ruin the set. When you take it off, always be sure to put it back onto the wig block if you have one. And now a plea on behalf of the wardrobe and wig department — never, never attempt to brush through a set wig without permission. It takes time to style a wig and if you do this you may have an expensive disaster on your hands. There is a right way to put on and take off a hair lace wig, which I shall describe below.

Before you begin you will need:

- a stocking cap

- spirit gum

1. Begin by putting a stocking cap over your own hair. If your hair is very long or very short, see the advice on pages 60-63. Make sure that all your hair is tucked into the cap.

2. You can put the wig on yourself or get help. If, as in the photos overleaf, you have

help, hold the front edge of the wig and pull it down onto your forehead first so that it can be stretched over your head. If you do this solo, you need to hold the front with one hand and the back with the other. Lift the wig onto your head, again starting at the forehead, and then carefully pull it over the stocking.

3. You now need to glue the hair lace flat to your head — if you don't do this it will show under the light.

There should be two little flaps of net just in front of your ears if the wig is on straight. Put a little dash of spirit gum on the skin under each flap and press the lace onto it, stretching it downwards as you do this. This will secure the wig front and tighten the lace across the forehead making it invisible to the audience.

4. Press the flaps against your skin for a few minutes to allow the spirit gum to dry. If your part involves a lot of action it may be wise to pin the back of the wig to the stocking cap with bobby pins for extra security.

Removing the wig

Pull the hair lace carefully away from your skin (you may need to dissolve the adhesive with remover first). Hold the front and back of the wig and lift it forward off your head. Clean off the gum on your face with spirit gum remover or surgical spirit.

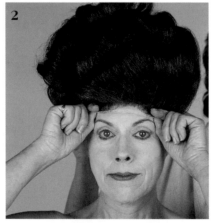

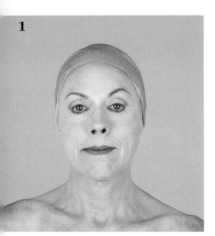

The finished effect

Synthetic wigs & hairpieces

Most theatrical wigs are real hair but an increasing number are made from a combination of real hair and acrylic fibers. These usually need fitting and are only available from specialists, but you can buy acrylic and monofiber wigs off-the-peg in many big stores. They are much cheaper than real hair wigs and, for simple purposes, easier to look after. The difference is that they are not hand-knotted, come on a stretch-base and fit most normal head sizes. The size of the wig can usually be adjusted by two little pieces of elastic at the back. Wigs like these are on sale in many large department stores.

Another difference between these and hair lace wigs is the heavier front edge which makes it difficult to style them back off the forehead.

You can wash and set them easily yourself, but beware of using heated rollers or tongs on this type of wig. The most useful styles for theatre are the softly curled mid-length ones which can be set into many different shapes.

You will find lots of hairpieces available in acrylic and monofiber, ranging from chignons right through to long switches and back extensions.

Cleaning the wigs

Most of these wigs can be hand-washed with lukewarm water and a gentle shampoo. Rinse well and, unless you are setting the wig, shake it and put it onto a block to dry naturally — you can speed up the process with a hairdryer.

ACRYLIC WIG TIP

✳ Conditioning is a waste of time — this isn't real hair!

How to put on a stretch-base wig

Unless your hair is quite short you will need to use a wig net or stocking cap to cover it before you start. If you don't do this your own hair will keep slipping out from under the wig. Because synthetic wigs have stretchy bases you will probably need to adjust the little elastics inside the back of the wig. There will either be little hooks to help you or, more usually, velcro. You generally can't tell if this is necessary until you try the wig on for the first time and then you can loosen or tighten the elastic according to your head size. You put this type of wig on in a different way to a hair lace one. You will need to hold it at the back and lift it down over your forehead (you will look seriously primitive at this point!) and then stretch it back over your own hair. Don't try putting it on from the back of your head first or you will push your own hair — and the wig net — forward and get into a mess. Once the wig is securely on your head, release your ears from beneath it and move the wig up your forehead to the correct position.

Is the wig on straight? You can check by feeling the edge just above your ears – there should be two little shaped bits there.

Finally, pin it to your own hair just above your ears. You remove the wig in the same way that you would remove a hair lace one — lifting it off from the back of your head (remember to remove the bobby pins first).

WIG TIP

✳ Because of their elastic base these wigs can lift up at the back. This problem can be solved by securing it to the stocking cap by using bobby pins at the back of your neck.

D.I.Y. wig net ~ how to make one

This is so simple to do that I often wonder why anyone buys one.

All you need is:

- an ordinary stocking
- scissors

The stocking will need to be fairly robust so I am afraid that 10 denier will not do. A friend who wears stockings and is willing to pass on her laddered ones would be a wonderful wig net source because the part you need — the top — rarely ladders.

To gauge how much stocking you will need to cut off I suggest that you pull it over your head and tuck your hair in. Then tie a knot in it on the top of your head and cut away the rest. You now have a perfectly good wig net.

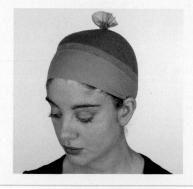

NET TIP

✳ To avoid hysterical laughter or being mistaken for a bank robber, it may be best to do this when you are alone.

Toupees & half-wigs

A toupee or half-wig can make a big difference to a balding actor. Often, as with our model, it can make him appear more youthful. A half-wig covers the whole front of the head, whereas a toupee is smaller and may just fill in the gap behind the front hair or disguise a receding hairline. Toupees are normally held in place with toupee tape which is double-sided and sticks to the natural skin and the false piece. The other type of toupee, which fills in the front hair, is usually made with a hair lace front which is glued to the skin with little dabs of spirit gum (see pages 55-56).

However, it may need toupee tape as well. Toupee tape is often referred to in this context as a "plaster". Theatrical half-wigs are usually made on a hair lace base with a net front, so unless there is a possibility of disturbing them they don't usually need toupee tape.

This hair lace half-wig is very dark, so to make it appear more believable I have darkened the model's eyebrows and added eye lines and mascara. With hair this dark you would have a noticeable beard shadow which I have created by stippling the jawline with cake eyeliner.

Toupee tape

This double-sided tape, which holds toupees and half-wigs to your head, has other uses as well. Use it when you need to put on or take off a moustache very quickly during a show (you can buy specially shaped pieces for this purpose). I have also used it to prevent a stretch-base wig from rising up at the back of an actor's head. A strip of tape can be placed horizontally across the edge of the stocking cap to hold the wig in place.

Wigs & very short hair

You would suppose that there would be little problem wearing a wig over short hair like this wouldn't you? Well, you would be wrong — although you won't have to secure masses of hair under it or need to use a stocking cap to hold the hair flat to the head, there is a problem nevertheless. This is the problem — with very short hair there is nothing to attach the wig to for security. This means that in action scenes or during dance sequences or even romantic clinches, there is a strong possibility that the wig will fall off.

So what is the solution? Well, you need to use tiny wig springs like these. You attach them to the hair, and once the wig is on you can push hairpins through the wig and underneath the springs to hold it safely to your head.

How to use wig springs

You will need:

- 4 springs

- 2 strong hairpins

- more pins to push through the wig

First of all you will need to thread hairpins through the little rings at each end of the spring. Holding the pins in two hands, stretch the spring as far as you can and place it against your hair as our model is doing. Relax the spring, which should now be caught firmly in the hair, and remove the hairpins.

Place one spring in the front of the hair, one at each side and one at the back of the head.

Finally, put your wig on and using short, strong pins, push them through the wig base and under the springs. The wig should now be completely secure to your head.

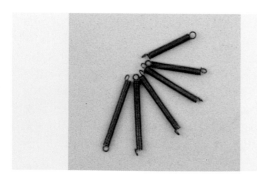

> ### *SPRING TIP*
>
> ❋ The minus with wig springs is removing them — you can lose hair if you are careless. Always put the pins back into the ends and stretch the spring, then carefully lift it away from your head. Don't try to just pull them out unless you enjoy pain!

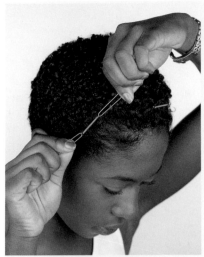

Stretching the spring to catch
the hair

The spring secured in the hair

Wig securely in place

61

Wigs & long hair

Long hair can be a real problem when you are asked to wear a wig. What do you do with all that length? Watching actresses who don't know, I have observed that they either twist it up onto the top of their head or into a rough pleat at the back. Both ways can cause the head to appear deformed once the wig is on. Other problems can arise with hair lace wigs as these have no "give". If the hair is not really flat to the head, the wig will rise up or, worse still, look like a Buckingham Palace guard's Busby on the top of your head.

Sometimes I have seen an actress try to put on a wig without using a stocking cap. What happens then is that a percentage of the hair falls down and has to be stuffed back up — eventually this hair will continue to slip out during the show.

So what should you do? First of all, I have to say that it is much easier to fit long hair under a synthetic wig, which has an elastic base, than a hair lace one, especially if you haven't had a wig fitting — it is a nightmare if the wig is tight. To successfully fit a short wig over long hair, that hair has to be as flat to your head as you can get it. If your hair is shorter than our model's you could try pincurling the whole head (see page 32 for instructions), but pincurls that have been badly done will give a lumpy effect under a sleek wig. The best solution, I think, is to wrap the hair. Here is how you do this:

You will need:

- a stocking top
- a brush and comb
- bobby pins
- metal clips (preferably long ones)
- hairspray or gel

1. Brush your hair back smoothly and clip the sides just above your ears. Using the comb make a center parting right down the back of your head. Tuck one side out of the way over your shoulder.

2. Starting from the ear, sweep the other side across the back of your head and up to above your other ear. Try to ensure that the hair is as smooth as possible and then pin it securely (at this point you may have to remove the clip on that side). Spray the smoothed hair well.

3. Sweep the other side across to your other ear, grip and spray. Comb the end pieces across the front of your head and secure them, making sure that there are no bumpy bits. Spray the whole head and then remove metal clips.

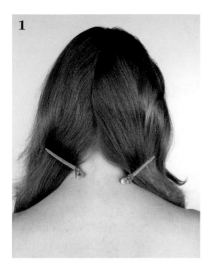

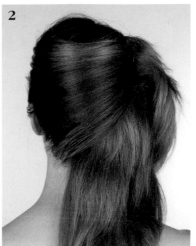

Once you have finished you can put your hands inside the stocking cap and stretch it carefully over your wrapped hair. Now pop your wig on.

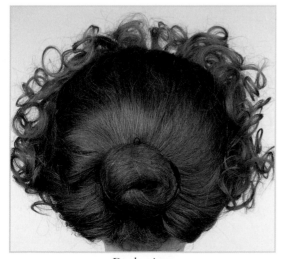

Back view

Wig in place

Budget wigs ~
using a fashion wig from a department store

Sometimes a production budget precludes professional wig hire. If so, all is not lost — it is amazing what can be achieved with a basic synthetic fashion wig.

However, be warned, it has to be a curly wig. Straight wigs are manufactured to remain straight and you will have enormous difficulties if you try to restyle one. The style I have chosen for demonstration purposes is shoulder length and reminiscent of the late 1970s and early 1980s. It is very versatile.

There are two ways of setting a synthetic wig. You can either damp it down and set it with rollers or clips, letting it dry naturally or drying it with a hairdryer, or you can set it while dry using spray gel to hold the shape in place. Either way you will need a wig block and a wig clamp. Without these you will have great difficulty unless, of course, you style the

wig on someone's head, but it is much easier to do this on a block. You need to attach the clamp to a table edge, fit the block onto it and pin your wig onto the block. You will need long wig pins for this, although I have successfully used glass-headed dress-making pins when I haven't had any to hand. Once the wig is securely pinned to the block, you can angle the clamp to suit your purpose.

Here are two very different period styles, one male and one female, that you can easily achieve with this bouffant fashion wig.

To style a wig like this you will need:

- hairbrush and tail comb
- hairpins and bobby pins
- firm hold spray gel
- a block, wig clamp and wig pins

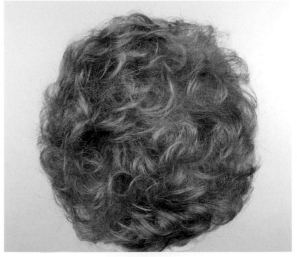

Here is the wig before styling

Neither of these styles require wetting the wig down. That is the joy of a curled wig like this — it is so easily styled. Begin by ensuring that your wig is securely pinned to the block, otherwise it may fly off.

18th century gentleman of fashion's wig

This is a fairly typical wig of the period and it is interesting to compare our D.I.Y. version with the professional wig on page 99. You will need two extra items for this:

- a covered elastic band

- a large black satin or velvet bow

1. Brush through the wig carefully, holding it at the front with the flat of one hand.

2. Now separate a front section from the rest (the tail comb is great for doing this).

3. Separate a section on each side of the wig and pin them out of the way.

4. Brush the rest of the hair back and down. Secure it in a low pony tail at the base of the wig. Use the covered elastic band for this.

5. Backcomb the front section and roll it back from the forehead. Tuck the ends under and pin to hold it in place.

6. Taking each side section at a time, divide them into two horizontal sections and backcomb them. Smooth the hair and roll up into two sausage shapes starting with the top section. (Use metal clips to hold that in place whilst you do the bottom sausage.)

7. Check the shapes and secure with bobby pins at each end. Then check that the two sides balance and spray the whole wig *well*.

8. Tie a large bow across the back and secure it with bobby pins.

Dressed wig

Typical back view

NOTE: This style could be sprayed with white hairspray for a more formal 18th century wig.

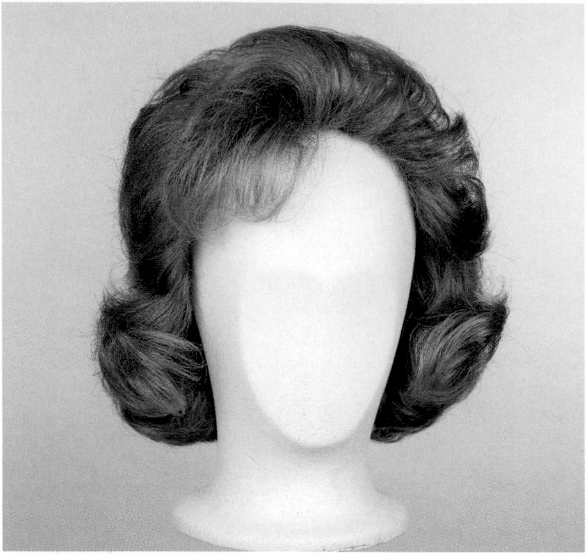

1950s style

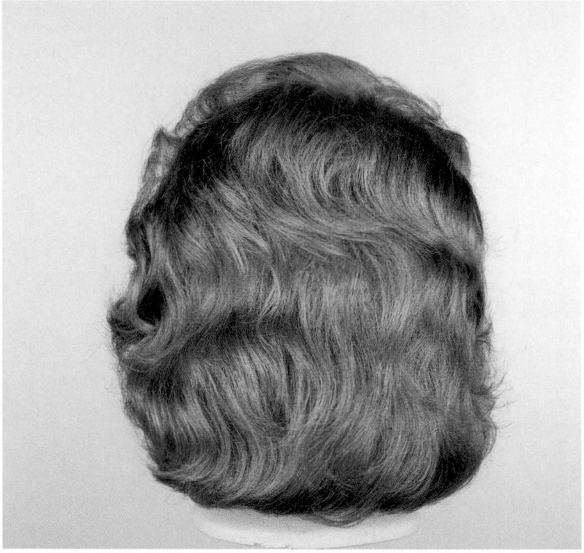

Back view

1950s everyday fashion style

This is quite a nostalgic style for me, as I used to wear my hair like this as a teenager. It is very simple to do.

1. Start by carefully brushing the wig through, then backcomb the top to give height.

2. Using the brush, smooth the hair back. Sweep one side forward in a soft wave onto the forehead and clip with a metal clip into position.

3. Brush the sides and back downwards and, using the tail comb, backcomb them. At this point you can form soft waves across the back with your fingers (see photograph on page 29) and clip them.

4. With the brush, smooth the back and the sides over your other hand and turn them under.

5. Clip the sides about halfway up to flatten them to the head and backcomb the hair below that. Shape into soft waves curving back off the cheeks.

6. Spray well and lift any areas that look a bit flat with your tail comb end. Remove clips.

WIG TIP

❋ Always hold the front of a wig with the flat of your hand when brushing through the fibers or you will tear them.

False eyelashes

Whenever glamour is part of a female role, false eyelashes come into their own. Of course, it isn't only women who use them — where would drag queens be without them? Also, many of the fashion faces of the past require them. I am thinking particularly of the 1960s, when two or sometimes three pairs of lashes were an integral part of the eye make-up of top models and every fashion-conscious girl wore at least one pair. The elegant look of the 1930s is completed with a pair of spiky lashes and a Restoration beauty needs fluffy ones to flutter over her fan.

For older actresses false lashes are a godsend. The fold of skin which often develops at the outer corners of the eyes makes eyeline extensions impossible to draw, but false eyelashes solve the problem by lifting the eye corners and making the eyes look younger. If you are fair-haired and find yourself cast as a Mediterranean or Hispanic, the contrast between your black wig and the fairness of your eyes can be a problem, but good eyelines and the correct false lashes will give you a believable Latin look.

However, I know that many people find lashes difficult to work with so here are some helpful hints.

Buying false eyelashes

• If you can go to a professional theatre or film make-up stockist, they have a much bigger range to choose from. If you can't do that, the big stockists have catalogs that they can send to you.

• If you just want to enhance your own, choose the television ones — they aren't too long and they won't overpower your eyes.

• You can buy separate tubes of lash glue in larger sizes.

Before you put them on

• Trim the lashes with sharp scissors, working with an angled snipping movement rather than cutting along the ends. They should be short at the inner corners with the longest hairs not quite reaching the outer ends.

• Lashes are easier to apply if you cut them into two or three sections. Sometimes you only need half-lashes at the outer ends of the eyes.

Trim lashes inwards

• Finish the whole eye make-up *including* mascara before putting on the lashes, otherwise you will disturb them.

• Make sure that the skin of your eyelids close to your eyelashes is well powdered or the adhesive will not stick and the lashes will come adrift.

Putting the lashes on

Whole lashes

• If you have large fingers or feel ham-fisted use a pair of tweezers to hold them.

• Squeeze a blob of glue onto the back of your hand and run the lash edge through it, ensuring that you have a good amount on each end.

• Stick your chin up and look down into the mirror. Place the lash as close as you can behind your own lashes, securing the center first, then the inner corner and finally the outer end. Roll the skin of your eyelid gently over the lash root with a finger.

• If the lash feels heavy, put a finger under your eyelashes and close your eye gently onto it. This should make the lash feel more comfortable.

• Carefully mascara the real and false lashes together. If any glue shows, redo your eyelines.

Half and cut lashes

Work in exactly the same way as for whole lashes — it's just easier in short sections.

False eyelashes for 20th century productions

As I have already indicated, false eyelashes can be very helpful in giving a more authentic feel to some period fashion make-ups. This is particularly true for some decades of the 20th century. Here are the decades in question:

1930s

The fashionable eye make-up of this decade, with its high arched eyebrows, emphasized bone structure. False lashes add to the effect by highlighting the roundness of the eyes. The correct lashes should be long and spiky but widely spaced. I have used my lash tip here (see opposite page) and lifted the outer end of the lash slightly above the eye corner.

1940s

The emphasis in the eye make-up of this time was still very much on the eyebrows, so false lashes need to look well spaced but quite natural. These are television lashes which are slightly thicker towards the outer ends. I have shortened the lash length at the inner corner of the eye.

1950s

Eyelines became fashionable in the 50s. A half-lash used from center lid to the outer corner will help to recreate the 'doe-eyed' look of the period. Marilyn Monroe was a fan of half-lashes.

1960s

This is the great decade for false lashes. No really fashion-conscious girl went without them. Often they wore two pairs on the top and one pair underneath the eyes. You will need thick heavy lashes to recreate this look, but be sure to trim them to suit your own eyes or they will obscure them.

After the 1960s false eyelashes gradually went out of fashion.

Cleaning false lashes

After every couple of uses you will need to remove the build-up of glue and mascara on the lashes. The best method of doing this is by laying them flat on a piece of damp cotton wool and using a wet cotton bud to work along the lashes, taking care not to push any off the ends. Then hold the lashes with a finger across the length and gently pick off the glue (sometimes tweezers can be helpful for this). If your lashes lose their curl, wrap them around a pencil and roll it up tightly in a piece of paper. Secure with an elastic band and leave overnight.

Lashes for African-American skins

If you are African-American you may find new lashes too straight in comparison to your own. Try the curling tip above but using a narrow pencil. It should make the curl of the lashes a little tighter which will make them easier to mingle with your own.

> ### *LASH TIP*
>
> ❋ Don't take the outer end of the false lash right down to the outer corner of the eye, or the lash can look droopy.

69

How to apply facial hairpieces securely

The key to ensuring that facial hairpieces remain safely glued to your face is preparation. There can be nothing more disturbing for an actor in full flow than to feel his moustache slipping. The stories are legion of people turning their backs to the audience to palm one or kissing their leading lady and leaving it on her top lip. But proper preparation will mean that this will never happen to you. So before sticking on your beard or moustache you need to do two things — tone your face and apply a foundation layer of spirit gum.

Let's begin with toning. This means using a lotion that tightens up the pores just like aftershave but also removes sticky moisture from the surface which could disturb the false piece. If you are a man who always shaves just before a performance and then uses aftershave, that will do the same thing. However, many men don't and so a toner, which is more gentle, is needed. Buying one can be confusing because the cosmetic houses call them by different names — Skin Freshener, Tonic, Toning Lotion — but they all do the same job and are the same thing.

Put some on a piece of cotton wool, pat it over your face and let it dry. Then put on your make-up base. I hope you are using one, because you will look much better on stage if you do. Now apply the foundation layer of spirit gum.

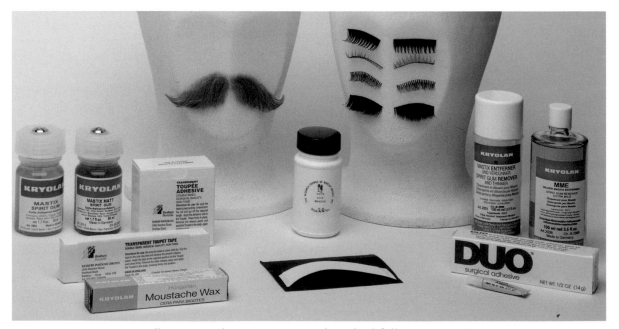

Adhesives and spirit gums are described fully on page 22

The foundation layer of spirit gum

The reason why moustaches, and sometimes beards, fall off is because sweat disturbs the spirit gum holding the pieces on. There is a simple solution: paint a layer of spirit gum where the piece is to go and let it dry completely ***before you even think about gluing it on***. This will prevent the sweat from coming through and loosening the false piece.

Now let's apply the false pieces:

Moustaches

After the foundation layer of glue has dried, paint another layer over it and press your moustache onto your top lip starting at the center. It is helpful to stretch your lip as you do this. When the moustache is centered, press down the sides taking care that you haven't glued them across your smile.

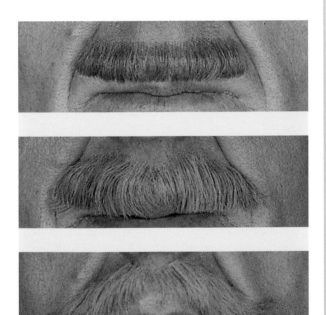

Different moustache shapes

Waxing moustaches

When tapered moustaches like the Kaiser style (page 103) were fashionable, men used wax to achieve the perfect shape. More recently, some movie stars, like Vincent Price, have worn waxed moustaches. Wax could also be used to point a goatee beard.

You can find this product at larger theatrical make-up stockists. To use it, take a little onto two fingers and smooth it along the moustache ends to point or twirl them.

A word about spirit gums

Male top lips and chins are notoriously sensitive areas. Poor things, how could they be otherwise since they are constantly being shaved? This, combined with the use of spirit gum, can make the skin sore over a run of shows or during filming. So I suggest that if you will be wearing a false moustache or beard for some time, you look for, indeed search for, medicated spirit gum which is kinder to your skin if it is inflamed. In the unlikely event that you are sensitive to medical spirit gum go to a pharmacy that stocks surgical appliances, or a major theatrical make-up store, and ask for Duo adhesive which is a latex glue. I am told that it is virtually impossible to be allergic to it.

Water soluble spirit gum

I'm sure this has its uses but it is not suitable for sweaty top lips. Use this and your moustache will probably fall off.

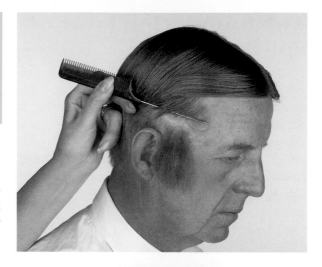

Side whiskers

I hate the way that when these are stuck on badly there is always a little gap between them and the real hair. You can avoid this by growing the hair above them a little longer.

Before you begin, see page 71 which explains how using an extra layer of spirit gum can prevent sweat from building up under whiskers.

1. Comb the hair up like this and hold it with a pin or clip. Glue the false side whiskers as close to the hairline as possible, making sure that they come right up to the roots of the clipped hair.

2. Remove the clip and carefully comb your side hair over the edge of the false whiskers.

NOTE: Obviously it is impossible to hide the edge perfectly if the hair at the sides of your face is very short.

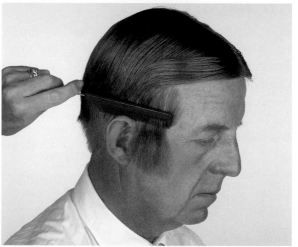

Beards

You follow the same routine, making sure that for big beards you have painted spirit gum under your chin as well.

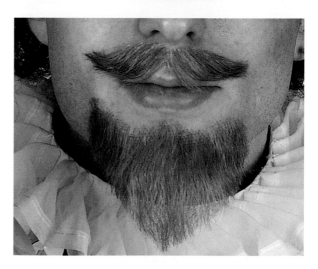

False eyebrows

There are some characters like, for example, Shakespeare's Falstaff, which seem to demand false eyebrows. To use a pair of good quality hair lace brows you will need first of all to make your own as flat to your skin as possible. If you don't do this you will have terrible problems attaching them.

You will need:

- spirit gum
- liquid latex
- a little dish
- a toothbrush
- a ³/₈ inch brush (optional)

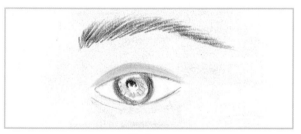

Before

1. Brush spirit gum through the brow working inwards towards your nose. This ensures that the hair becomes well coated. Then quickly work the hairs *upwards* with the toothbrush, flattening them well to your skin.

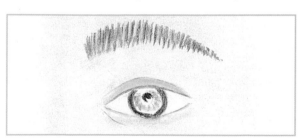

Pour a little latex into the dish and with your finger or the brush, smooth it over the glued brow. I prefer to use my finger — it is much easier to clean afterwards. When dry, add a further layer and let that dry also. Powder.

2. If the false brows are shorter or thinner than your own you will now need to cover the brow area and latex with a cream or stick foundation (see below).

Powder it, then paint spirit gum where the new brow is to go and press the false one firmly into position. For a cheap version see page 79.

Fair, fine brows

You can buy eyebrow mastic in a stick which you rub through the brows to flatten them. You will then need to powder them before applying the new brows.

WARNING

✳ Spirit gum dries very quickly.

✳ Latex also dries quickly and goes into stringy little balls if you are slow.

Take one man &
three moustaches

I suspect that many actors are unaware of the difference the shape of a moustache can make to the way they look. It is actually a very simple way of adding character to a role. As you will see when you come to the Period Styles section, it can also be an important factor in creating the look of another time.

To demonstrate, I have chosen three quite different moustache styles and, to complete the picture, combed the model's hair differently to complement each one and added costume to suit each character.

Here is our man as he looks in real life. You will notice one interesting thing as he changes character — despite the differing shapes, he actually looks older with the moustaches on. You will need to bear this in mind, as moustaches do tend to make all men look a little older.

Moustache one

When I put this moustache on our model it immediately reminded me of Bertie Wooster, one of P. G. Wodehouse's wonderful characters and the rarefied world of the English aristocrat which he exemplified. So I parted the hair in the middle and chose a 1920s jacket and bow-tie, the sort of outfit that a country gent would have worn at the time.

Moustache two

This one took me straight back to all those films about the Second World War and the Battle of Britain, when the gallant few of the R.A.F. won the war of the skies against the Luftwaffe. I saw this as a Wing Commander's moustache and so I made a side parting in the model's hair and slicked it back firmly. This type of man would have worn a cravat with his casual clothes when off duty.

Moustache three

Well, I don't think that I have to say who this moustache reminded me of, but Adolf Hitler's was actually quite a bit shorter and longer under the nose. Nevertheless it immediately dictated the hairstyle. The dark suit somehow adds to the sinister effect of the moustache. It must be said, however, that many men wore a shape like this in the 1930s.

TOP LIP TIP

❊ If your top lip gets sore try an old fashioned remedy — lacto-calamine lotion. It is wonderful for healing top lips and shaving rashes — and it's cheap!

Crêpe hair

Also called crêpe wool, this has been used in theatres for centuries. It is an inexpensive way to make beards and moustaches, side whiskers and queues when all else fails. I am sure that most men reading this will, at some time or another, have had terrible crêpe hair moustaches put on them by enthusiastic drama teachers when they were at school. In point of fact, properly prepared it is a very useful product. The problem is that most people don't know how to use it properly. Let's begin by preparing it. The first important rule is that you never use it as it comes. It has to be pressed.

Preparing crêpe hair

To do this you will need:

• the crêpe hair

• a steam iron or ordinary iron with a damp cloth

1. Unravel the hair by pulling it downwards and away from the internal strings.

2. Lay the hair out on an ironing board and, if you are using an ordinary iron, cover it with the damp cloth (a handkerchief is good for this).

3. Carefully press the hair flat, stretching it as you iron. It should be completely flat when you have finished.

The hair is now ready for use. At this point you could mingle two colors together.

Loosened and ready to press

Hair as purchased

Ready for use

So, what can we use it for?

Several days' beard growth

You will need:

- prepared crêpe hair
- scissors
- a saucer
- wax beard stubble stick
- a soft sponge

Rub the wax stick over your chin and top lip. Snip tiny pieces of crêpe hair into the saucer. Apply the snipped stubble to the waxed area with the sponge, pressing it into the wax. This will take a bit of practice.

Small David Niven style moustache

You will need:

- prepared crêpe hair
- spirit gum
- scissors
- a soft, dry sponge or velour puff
- a brush or pencil

Cut lengths of crêpe hair about 2–2½ inches long (shorter ones will be difficult to handle). Paint a line of spirit gum along your top lip and let it dry.

Paint another line of gum, feather out the crêpe hair and, starting in the middle (**1**), press it along the line until you reach the end, angling it naturally (**2**). Check that there are no hairs heading for your nose and, if there are, trim them away. With the brush or pencil, roll its length along the glued hair to force it into the glue. Finally trim the moustache to the desired length (**3**).

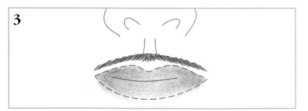

Adding to a real moustache or beard

You will need:

- prepared crêpe hair
- spirit gum
- scissors

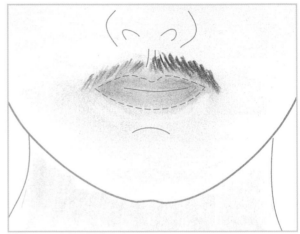

Cut lengths of crêpe hair to the required length and feather the hair out. Place spirit gum where you need to add the beard or moustache and carefully lay strands of crêpe hair among the real hair. Press firmly into place. Should the crêpe hair stand out from the rest, spray some hair gel onto your fingers and smooth it carefully back into position.

BEARD TIP

❊ Never attempt to comb the hair into place. You will pull it away from the glue.

Crêpe hair eyebrows

It is easy, if somewhat fiddly, to make crêpe hair eyebrows. Remember that before you begin you will need to block out your own, or, if they are fair, glue them flat with spirit gum (**1**) (see page 73).

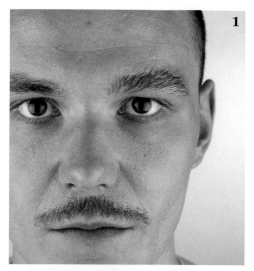

You will need:

- some prepared crêpe hair to match your hair or wig

- spirit gum

- hairspray or spray gel

- small scissors

- long handled make-up brush or pencil

If the new brows are to be above your own or shorter, make sure that you have made up over the blocked real ones and powdered the area (**2**).

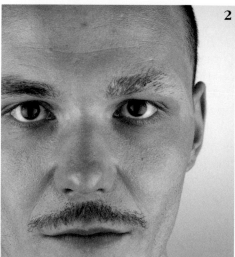

Cut the crêpe hair to a length that is short but easy to handle — you can always trim it later — feather it out and angle it to the way that it is supposed to be growing. Paint spirit gum halfway along the new brow position (don't paint it right across the brow now because it will dry before you reach the last bit). Take a small amount of hair and lay it in position on your browbone. Then take the brush handle or pencil and roll it over the hair roots to force them into the glue. Follow the same routine again, adding more hair until you get the shape that you require. Trim the hair as necessary and carefully smooth into position using a little hairspray or spray gel on your finger (**3**). Now do the other brow.

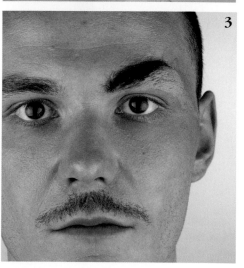

CRÊPE EYEBROW TIP

✳ You can use your finger to smooth a little spray gel over the crêpe hair to keep the false brow in shape.

✳ If you paint two layers of latex over the brow area after blocking out and glue the crêpe brows onto that, you will be able to reuse them a couple of times. Between uses, powder the back of the latex to prevent it from curling.

Making your own queue

for 18th century plays

What is a queue? Well, in the 18th century men wore wigs with the back hair long and tied in a low pony tail. At that time everything French was chic, so elegant men used the Gallic term "queue" — meaning a tail — to describe this style. These "queues" were worn long, short, divided into two tails and sometimes even covered with a small black bag. Men who couldn't afford wigs dressed their own hair into a queue. Since the plays of this period by writers such as Richard Brinsley Sheridan and John Gay are still widely performed, I thought it would be helpful to learn how to make your own queue just in case your own hair is too short to do this and there is no wig budget for your character. It is simple to do and, because you will use crêpe hair, cheap as well.

You will need:

• a length of prepared crêpe hair to match your own hair color as closely as possible (see page 76)

• scissors

• a needle

• black thread

• a length of 2-inch wide black ribbon in satin or velvet

1. The queue could be long or short, but basically it needs to be long enough to stretch from the center back of your head to just below your collar. You need to make sure that there is enough to do that *and* fold back on itself in a loop.

Queue back showing bobby pin positions

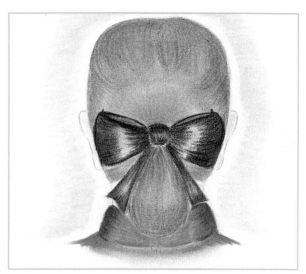

Queue in position

2. Now wrap the thread round the cut end tightly and knot it. You should have about 1 inch of cut hair sticking out above the thread.

3. Carefully loosen the loop to spread out the crêpe hair and make a soft full tail.

4. Make a nice large bow from the ribbon and trim the ends. Lay it flat on a table. Thread the needle and stitch the crêpe hair onto the back of the bow knot making sure that no bits show above it.

Attaching your home-made queue

Once you have made your queue you will need to attach it safely to your own hair.

You will need:

• a comb with narrow teeth

• bobby pins, both long and short

• hairspray

Go to page 34 to see how to backcomb hair, as you will need to backcomb the front to give the hair more volume and make it easier to handle. When you have done this, smooth your hair back from your forehead making sure that you leave a little height in the front.

Now comb the sides back behind your ears and hold them in place with short bobby pins. Spray your hair well to keep it in position.

Make a little curl with your finger in the center back hair and hold it in place with crossed bobby pins.

Put a long bobby pin through the knot of the bow at the back and slide the bow into place across the curl (you need to open the bobby pin to do this). Then slide a long pin through each end of the bow, and also your hair, to hold it securely to your head.

QUEUE TIPS

✱ You need to do this with clean hair — greasy hair won't backcomb.

✱ You can't attach a queue to very short hair.

Bald caps

I think that bald caps come under the brief of this book because they are often linked with wigs worn by some characters. For example, Lady Wishfort in the famous Restoration comedy *The Way of the World* is frequently played as bald but wearing a wig to hide it. Bald caps are difficult to put on properly if you don't know how. It is possible to make your own caps, but for our purposes I am talking about the ones that you buy ready-made from theatrical make-up stockists. Typically you will find three types available:

Latex
These are rubber caps that usually come in three sizes — small, medium and large. Ready-made latex caps are generally heavy-duty and ideal for a lot of hard wear. However, the edge of this type of cap is not easy to hide in a small theatre.

Glatzen
Plastic cap in one stretchable size. Glatzen is a stiffer material which is also fairly heavy-duty.

Pre-impression: *a thinner Glatzen cap*
This is the type of cap sold mainly to cover the hair when an actor is having their head cast in plaster. It is my personal favorite because it is so much easier to hide the front edge and make it look realistic. However, this cap is not as hard-wearing as the others and you must be careful not to tear it when you remove it.

Putting on a bald cap

I think it is virtually impossible to do this by yourself so this advice is written for your helper.

You will need:

• the cap (chose one slightly smaller than your head size)

• hairspray

• a small pair of scissors

• an eyebrow pencil

• spirit gum

• a tail comb

• a soft, dry sponge or velour puff

• adhesive tape

1. Begin by combing the hair away from the forehead and back behind the ears unless you have short hair. Spray it well with hairspray — you don't want to be battling with stray strands of hair whilst you are working. Ask the actor to hold the cap front edge and together carefully pull it over the head starting from the front. When you have finished, the front will be right down to the eyebrows, the ears inside it and there should be a long piece at the neck. Check that it is tight to the hair on the top of the head. At this point I tuck any stray hairs that have escaped back under the cap with the end of the tail comb and then tape the sides to the face as in the photograph.

2. Now use the eyebrow pencil to draw a wavy line across the forehead and down the sides of the cap, leaving a decent gap between it and the hairline. Check to see if the actor frowns a lot and, if so, make sure that the forehead line is above the frown lines. Go to the ears and draw a cutting line following the shape but well inside the actual ear edge.

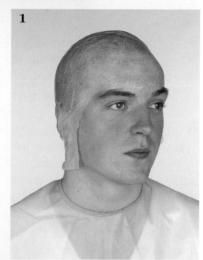

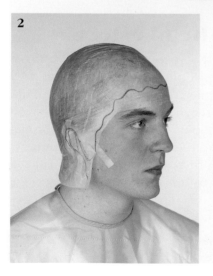

This is important because the cap must fit snugly around the ear. Join this line up with the wavy line, making a flap in front of the ear. Remove the tape, then carefully cut along the pencil line and discard the excess material. Bring the ears through the ear holes and see if the shape is comfortable. If not, cut away a little more cap until each ear feels comfortable. Leave the back as it is for now.

3. *(See photo overleaf)* Now you are going to glue the front. Before you start, check for any hair that is caught beneath it and push it back with the tail comb. Lift the cap front, paint spirit gum on the underlying skin and then firmly press the edge back into place using the sponge or puff. This will help to "disappear" the edge into the forehead. Allow a minute for the glue to dry and then start work on the side flaps. One by one, paint spirit gum under them and stretch them down and onto the gum. Ask your actor to hold each one in place whilst you do the other. Check to see if there is any wrinkling of the edge and if so peel the flap back and start again, stretching it down more firmly.

4. *(See photo overleaf)* When the front is really dry, ask the actor to drop their head right down as far as they can, holding the sides of the cap. Then stretch the back flap downwards as hard as you can with both hands. Ask the actor to lift their head and check if there are any wrinkles on the top of the head. If there are restretch; if not, ask them to drop their head again and, holding the flap in place with one hand, paint spirit gum on the neck beneath it and press the cap firmly onto it. *Hold for 2 or 3 minutes.* When *dry* the head can come up and you will be able to cut away any excess cap and glue the back edges down.

NOTE: It is very difficult to achieve a perfect back edge to a bald cap.

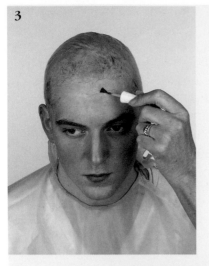

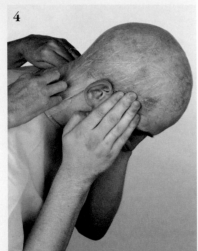

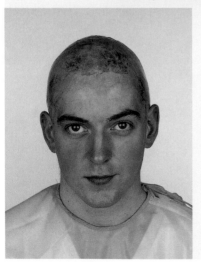

A finished cap ready for coloring

Coloring bald caps

If a cap has to last a long time it would be wise to use bald cap grease for coloring because other foundations can eat away the surface. But for a short run, cream-based foundations like paintsticks and cremestiks are excellent.

To color the cap you will require:

- bald cap grease or paintstick
- a sponge (slightly damp)
- translucent powder
- a half-inch brush

It is enormously helpful if the actor has a good even foundation on their face as this makes it much easier to match the cap to the skin. I generally find that you need more than one color to cover the cap so I tend to mix a couple on the back of my hand and then stipple them over the cap. Often a little brown-red (e.g. Kryolan EF9 Supercolor) added to the base tone is helpful. When you have achieved a good cover you may need to paint a little more across the front edge with a brush. Once you have finished, powder the head lavishly with translucent powder.

Shaved head effect

I think the best way to achieve this is to color the cap as described above, powder it well and then stipple cake make-up or cake liner in dark brown where you need the shaved effect. You could also use a dark brown cream make-up to do this, that will then need re-powdering. In both cases you will get the best effect by using an open-textured sponge to stipple.

A colored cap

Adding hair

It is possible to glue crêpe hair to a bald cap. Depending on the effect you require you can use straightened or curly crêpe hair. Be sure to do this using mat spirit gum and, unless you are really good at laying hair, I strongly suggest that you only do it for little tufts or the effect of serious hair loss, otherwise the result will be unconvincing.

Removing the cap

By the end of a show you will be longing to just tear the cap off your head but don't! Here is how you should remove it.

You will need:

• spirit gum remover or, if you have run out of that, surgical spirit will do but it stings

• cotton wool or cotton buds

Gently pull one flap away from your skin and soak a piece of cotton wool or a bud in spirit gum remover. Rub this under the cap edge, gradually lifting it away from your head as you do. When you have loosened the whole front, lift the cap back off your head and dissolve the glue under the back edge. Lift the cap away.

Looking after your cap

After you have taken it off, turn it inside out and dry off any sweat. Powder the inside well with face powder or talc. If you can, keep it on a block for safety. I was once involved with a West End production in London where an actress left her bald cap on her dressing table in the theatre and by accident a cleaner, thinking it was rubbish, threw it away. The actress didn't discover this until the next performance and panic ensued as you can imagine. So keep your cap safe.

Over a series of performances the spirit gum will build up on the cap edge. This build-up can usually be removed with spirit gum remover.

BALD CAP TIP

❋ Never use pins under a cap — they will split it. If you need to hold hair up under a cap, adhesive tape is the answer.

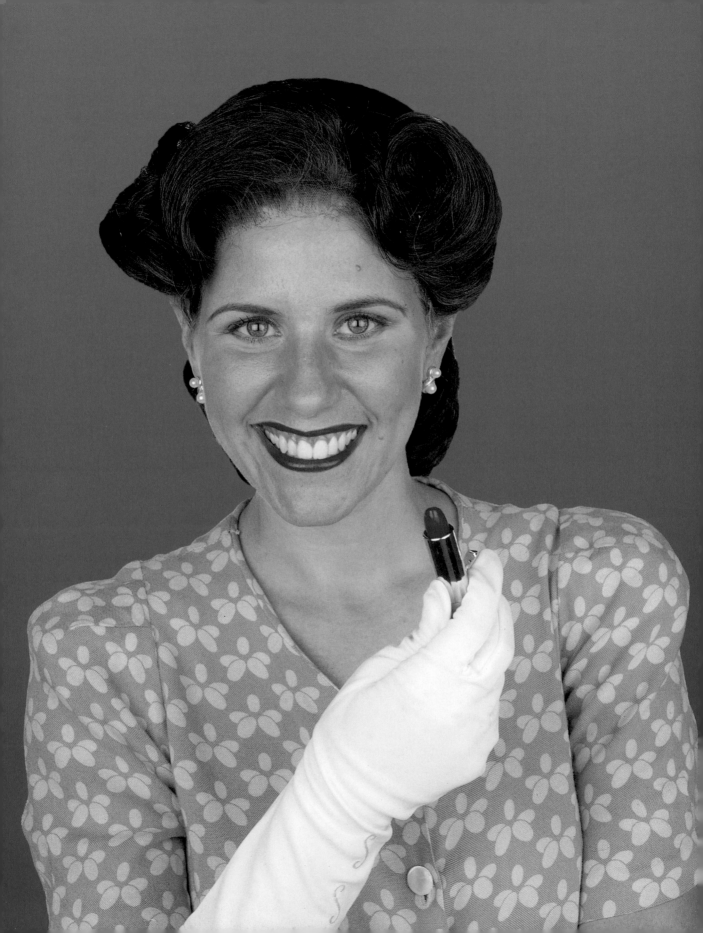

Section Three

Period Styles

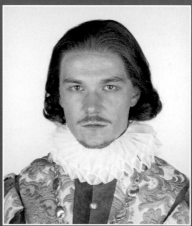

Period styles

When a production is set in a past era with accurate costumes, you will need to think carefully about the hairstyles of the period and men will need to check if their character would have worn facial hair of some description. Neglect this and you can easily look out of period, almost as if you are wearing the wrong head. I remember a few years ago, seeing a beautifully styled Noël Coward play in London's West End. Everyone was correctly coifed and made up for the 1930s except one young actor whose blond hair flopped over his eyes in a most inappropriate way for the time. It made him look far too modern as well as unfinished in his elegant costumes.

Indeed, for some plays and shows the correct hair and make-up is vital for the look of the piece. Just imagine Sheridan's *The School for Scandal* without its powdered wigs and patches, or the girls of the Fandangle Ballroom in *Sweet Charity* minus their tarty 60s hairstyles and false eyelashes. Wouldn't that be disappointing? So when you find yourself cast in a period, a little research will be needed and this can be quite time consuming. You may find the look, but could you achieve it with your own hair or would a wig be more appropriate? If you are male, which moustache or beard would be right for your character? To help you, this part of the book covers the fashionable style of the past, beginning with the Elizabethans and finishing

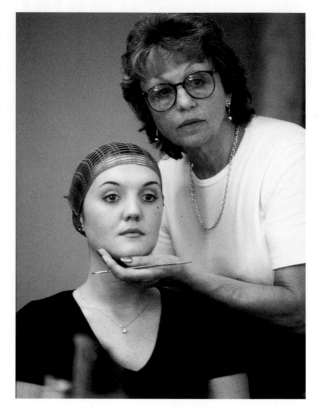

in the 1970s. Each section describes the hairstyles in fashion at the time and offers suggestions on how to achieve them effectively. Where necessary you will be referred back to previous chapters for detailed techniques. If you wish to learn the correct make-up for each period may I refer you to my book *Period Make-up for the Stage step-by-step*. The right hairstyle with the wrong make-up would be such a pity.

The Elizabethans
1533 ~ 1603

The Queen's active support of drama (in 1583 she formed her own theatrical company "Queen Elizabeth's Men") saved it from increasing religious prejudice. In the winter of 1601-2 ten new plays were produced at the court and choristers of the Queen's chapel were regularly loaned to play female roles in the intervals of masques and spectacles. It was during her reign that the leading actor of the day, Richard Burbage, built London's Globe Theatre where most of William Shakespeare's plays had their premieres. Elizabeth was present at the first performance of *A Comedy of Errors* and guest of honor at the wedding of Lord Derby when *A Midsummer Night's Dream* had its debut. Christopher Marlowe and Ben Jonson also established themselves as playwrights at this time.

Of course, Shakespeare's plays are still immensely popular although not always set in this period. Plays by his contemporaries such as *Dr. Faustus* by Marlowe and *Every Man in his Humour* by Jonson, are still firmly in the repertoire. Other popular productions set in this period include Johann Christoph Friedrich von Schiller's opera *Mary Stuart* and Robert Bolt's *Vivat, Vivat Regina!*

Elizabethan women

It was at this time that fashionable women began to uncover their hair in public and that the vogue for fashion wigs began. The center-parted hair, familiar to us from the portraits of the wives of Henry VIII and his daughter Mary Tudor, gave way to hair dressed back and high from the forehead, often worn over rats (in those days these were horsehair pads). But the keynote style of this period was dictated by Queen Elizabeth I who, after losing her own hair, took to wearing tightly curled auburn wigs which became progressively higher. History tells us that she possessed a large number of these meticulously curled wigs. The ladies of the Court hastened to copy the style using their own hair but many of them gave up and also took to wearing wigs. Hair was dyed saffron or auburn as a compliment to her and some ladies sprinkled theirs with gold dust.

Mary, Queen of Scots, Elizabeth's great rival, also had an array of auburn wigs and wore them constantly, so it came as a great shock to observers at her execution when the wig fell from her severed head to reveal short gray hair.

Generally in plays of this period you would be given a wig to wear. However, you could recreate the look on layered hair using very small rollers or pincurls across the front and top of the head, but keeping the back smooth. The back is usually taken into a small bun but this is often not seen as it is usually covered by a small cap or caul. At other times it is hidden by the elaborate ruffs and collars which were in fashion at that time.

ALSO SEE

❋ page 27: Designing the pli for a hairstyle

❋ page 30: Rollers — how to use them

❋ page 32: Pincurls — how to achieve the perfect curl

❋ page 39: Making a bun

Elizabethan men

At this time fashionable men generally wore their hair brushed back from the forehead and short in front of the ears. It varies at the back from quite short, as worn by Elizabeth's great favorite Robert Dudley, Earl of Leicester, to just below the ears as favored by her Chief Minister, Robert Cecil. Facial hair was in fact, more interesting. Long pointed beards became fashionable with older courtiers and bishops who wore theirs divided into "swallow tails". Moustaches were grown with downward ends, sometimes with long points like that of Sir Walter Raleigh, the discoverer of the New World.

However, Court dandies, like Nicholas Hilliard, the Queen's miniaturist, begged to differ. As well as pointed moustaches they chose shorter goatee style beards and styled their hair into a riot of auburn curls as a compliment to the Queen. Some grew a long side lock which they wore tied with a ribbon. They often dyed their beards and moustaches too. As in all fashionable society there were mavericks. Sir Phillip Sydney, the epitome of chivalry at Court, appears to have been clean-shaven whilst William Shakespeare, although, of course, not a courtier, looks very different in his pictures with his long bob and small lip beard. Ordinary men wore similar hairstyles to the fashionable elite and also copied their beards and moustaches.

ALSO SEE

❖ page 55: How to put on a hair lace wig

❖ page 58: How to put on a stretch-base wig

❖ page 70: How to apply facial hairpieces securely

Many of these styles are achievable with your own hair and facial hair, assuming that you have the time to grow a beard and moustache, or you could use false facial hair. Most actors playing an Elizabethan dandy would require a wig.

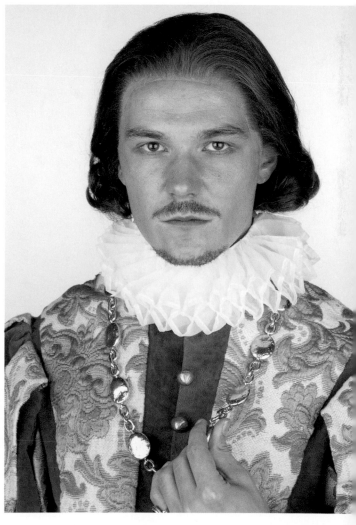

The Jacobeans & the early 17th century

Although James I only ruled England from 1603 until 1625, this is an important period in theatre terms. Shakespeare was still writing and many other important plays of the period, such as John Webster's *The Duchess of Malfi*, John Ford's *'Tis Pity She's a Whore* and Ben Jonson's *The Alchemist* are still widely performed today. Thomas Middleton's *A Game at Chess* made history at the Globe when it played for nine performances - this was theatre's first long run.

Jacobean women

By the beginning of the 17th century the wealth of the merchant class had grown and their women now had the money to follow fashion. The playwright Ben Jonson reiterates a common joke of the time in his piece *The Silent Woman* when he says of such a woman "all her teeth were made in Blackfriars, both her eyebrows in the Strand and her hair in Silver Street". As well as telling us that some women wore false eyebrows (popular again during the late Restoration), usually made

---

ALSO SEE

✳ page 30: Rollers — how to use them

✳ page 39: Making a bun

✳ page 52: Attaching a false hairpiece

from mouse or moleskin, this quote lets us know that wigs were still worn. However, this was to change as fashionable women abandoned tight Elizabethan curls for hair dressed softly back, often over rats and coiled into buns at the back of their heads. Soft curls framed the face and covered the ears, and many women wore part of their hair down at the back to the shoulder. Hair began to be decorated with ribbons and combs.

As long as you have shorter hair at the front and a reasonable length at the back, this style is easy to do yourself. If your hair is short you could add a false piece at the back.

Jacobean men

In the Jacobean period men still tended to wear their hair back from the face, sometimes short, sometimes longer. The King himself favored short hair, a shortish square chin beard and twirling moustachios. A contemporary etching of John Smith, the colonist, shows him with longer hair, a bushy full beard and a moustache reaching right across his face. The arrogant Duke of Buckingham is pictured in a drawing with a neat goatee.

What was no longer seen, except in the case of some older men, was the divided beard. French dandies would have copied the Duc d'Harcourt who sported a small braid around the front of one ear in which he wore a drop earring.

Unless you have a dearth of hair you will easily be able to create a short or long Jacobean hairstyle which can be accompanied by either a natural or false beard and moustache.

ALSO SEE

✻ page 44: Filling in a beard, moustache or side whiskers

✻ page 55: How to put on a hair lace wig

✻ page 70: How to apply facial hairpieces securely

The 17th century & the Restoration

Many of the Restoration comedies written during this period by such playwrights as William Wycherley, William Congreve, John Dryden and Sir John Vanbrugh, were stinging social comments on Society at that time. They are among the most enduring plays in the classical repertoire and if we add the wonderful French satires of Molière like *The Misanthrope, School for Wives* and *Tartuffe* this becomes an important time in theatrical terms.

The reign of Charles I 1625 ~ 1649

During this time women's hair remained much the same as before. The face was fringed with little soft curls and most women wore the back hair down. Some fashionable ladies wore pearl hair ornaments or ribbon loops as decoration; others dressed their side curls into wired soft ringlets.

Male hair was worn longer and most courtiers copied the King's neat little goatee beard and upturned shorter moustache. Foppish gentlemen affected "love locks", one or two pieces of hair worn forward and tied at the ends with ribbon.

Restoration women

With the ascension of Charles II to the English throne in 1660, Puritanism was swept away by the new King who brought from France, where he had lived in exile, all the extravagance of the French Court. Looking at the portraits of the Court beauties, Charles' many mistresses, there is a definite air of abandonment about their clothes and their hairstyles. Most have their hair parted in the middle with soft curls framing the face and a riot of more curls falling to below their shoulders. Sometimes the hair is caught behind the ears, sometimes not. The King's great favorite, Louise de Keroualle, whose appearance was captured in a wonderful portrait by Henri Gascar, absolutely typified the look of the age, with her hair quite wide at the sides, fashionably dark, artful curls on her forehead and the rest flowing around her shoulders. Curiously the color and shape is very reminiscent of the wigs of her royal lover. Nell Gwynn was sometimes painted with curly hair, but in the famous Lely painting of her the hair is shown falling more naturally in soft waves.

If you have long hair with some short pieces at the front, this is an easily achievable hairstyle. All that you will need to do is curl it, draw some of the side hair behind the ears with combs and create little curls in a flattering way around your hairline. Mid-length hair would require the addition of a long hairpiece but if your hair is short you would need a wig for this.

ALSO SEE

❖ page 27: Designing the pli for a hairstyle

❖ page 30: Rollers — how to use them

❖ page 33: Using a decorative comb

Restoration men

The fashion for male wigs arrived from the French court with Charles II. These extravagantly curled wigs hung as far as, and in some cases well below, the shoulders and were known as "full-bottomed". Their weight and the difficulty in cleaning them led to men shaving their own hair for comfort and the sake of hygiene.

The weight was such that the longer wigs were made with the length divided into three pieces, one worn at the back and the other two over the shoulders. Once it had been accepted at Court the fashion spread quickly. Samuel Pepys' diary provides a useful contemporary record of this fashion, and he agonized over whether to buy one of these wigs, his own hair being ample. But his desire to rise in society was keen and eventually he gave in, cut his hair and purchased a periwig for £3. During the plague years we find him commenting fearfully about the source of wig hair.

During this time moustaches thinned and beards fell out of favor, the latter appearing only as small tufts of hair under the bottom lip. Although the King's moustache came and went during his reign, many important men like the Duke of York, Sir Isaac Newton and Sir Christopher Wren (who built St. Paul's Cathedral) were completely clean-shaven.

You can easily grow the moustache and lip beard, paint them in or use crêpe hair. A full-bottomed wig would be required for a production of this period.

ALSO SEE

✳ page 44: Filling in a beard, moustache or side whiskers

✳ page 70: How to apply facial hairpieces securely

✳ page 76: Crêpe hair

The 18th century

Important plays of social comment on London society are set in this century. Contemporary writers like Richard Brinsley Sheridan, who wrote *The Rivals* and *The School for Scandal*, used sharp pens and eagle eyes to highlight the morals of the day. John Gay in his rumbustious *The Beggar's Opera* exposed the hardships of life at the other end of the social scale. In recent times Christopher Hampton's brilliant adaptation of Choderlos de Laclos's *Les Liaisons Dangereuses*, Peter Shaffer's *Amadeus* and Timberlake Wertenbaker's *Our Country's Good* have added further to plays of this period.

18th century women

In this, the Age of Enlightenment, it would seem that most fashionable women were anything but enlightened as they poisoned themselves with their red and white lead make-up and the powder that they used in their hair. Many great beauties of the time died from their desire to be fashionable. The latest styles of the Beau Monde were avidly copied by everyone who could afford them and magazines and fashion dolls took these styles to the farthest colonies. French fashion was everything and, following that, hair became more formally dressed again and initially shorter. Madame de Pompadour, Louis XV's mistress, wore hers drawn back from her face and secured in a soft bun, leaving some length coiled into soft ringlets over one shoulder.

However, this simplicity was not to last and, following the example of the French Court, hair gradually became higher and higher. This was achieved with the addition of horse hair pads, false hair and, in the case of the most extreme styles, wooden and iron cages over which the ladies' hair could be dressed. All hairstyles were powdered for formal occasions, usually with white lead but sometimes gray, blue or lilac. Marie Antoinette, perhaps the greatest fashion icon of her time, was known to use gold dust. She was also responsible for the addition of feathers, ribbons, models of ships and even windmills, as hair ornaments.

Dressing hair in this way was time consuming and expensive. As a result, most ladies of fashion kept the style in for several weeks which meant sleeping with the neck on a curved wooden block to protect the hair. Long-handled head scratchers (we know them now as back scratchers) became important accessories for every fashionable woman! Naturally women who had neither time nor money for this, or indeed sufficient hair, resorted to wigs.

The more elaborate styles of this period would obviously require a wig. If one is not forthcoming you could dress the fashion wig on page 64 into a feasible copy, adding side ringlets and spraying the whole thing white.

If your hair is quite long and the budget quite small, a reasonable approximation of the look can be achieved by backcombing the top hair into a high beehive, curling a small piece of hair in front of each ear and sweeping the length across the back and over one shoulder in soft ringlets. Hide the grips at the back with a festoon of ribbons.

ALSO SEE

❋ page 34: Backcombing or teasing hair

❋ page 64: Budget wigs

I have also achieved a reasonable effect on mid-length hair with the addition of a hair-piece at the back, and, when things are really desperate budget wise, used big bunches of ribbons with trailing ends to give the effect of length.

18th century men

Most 18th century men wore wigs if they could afford to. However, the full-bottomed fashions of the Restoration were gradually replaced by more practical shorter styles. The first important style was the "campaign wig" worn by military men.

This was replaced by the simpler "tie" wigs where the hair was drawn back from the face and tied at the back of the head with a black

ALSO SEE

❋ page 34: Backcombing or teasing hair

❋ page 65: 18th century gentleman of fashion's wig

❋ page 80: Making your own queue

ribbon. The tied back hair was called a "queue", which is French for a tail. The queue was also sometimes encased in a bag – these wigs were known as "bag wigs". If you couldn't afford a long wig you bought a short "Bob wig". Highly fashionable fops chose elaborate high wigs and the most famous of these, the Macaronis, had ones that rose to 18 inches in height. Wigs were generally powdered white or gray although there were brief fashions for other colors. Usually in productions of this period actors are given wigs to wear, but it is possible if you have a good amount of hair and some length to achieve the look of a simple wig. You would need to backcomb it and either tie it back or add a false queue.

Queen Victoria & the 19th century 1837 ~ 1901

Despite the prudery of the court of Victoria and Albert, this was the period that saw the rise of Music Hall — the people's theatre — which spawned great stars like Vesta Tilley, George Robey, Marie Lloyd and Dan Leno. Top music hall artists toured America and the Antipodes, and in 1868 a company of English chorus girls 'Lydia Thompson's British Blondes' introduced Burlesque to the USA with a show modeled on the popular minstrel shows. In England Gilbert and Sullivan's Savoy Operas, like *Patience*, lampooned late Victorian Society, whilst the legitimate theatre produced Ellen Terry and Henry Irving, the first actor to be knighted. There are many productions set in this era including Puccini's opera *La Bohème*; Feydean and Pinero's farces *A Flea in Her Ear* and *The Magistrate*; Turganev's *A Month in the Country*; and the musicals *The King and I* by Rodgers and Hammerstein, *Oliver* by Lionel Bart and *Sweeney Todd* by Stephen Sondheim.

Victorian women

During the time of Queen Victoria fashion became formal and decorous, modesty being considered essential for all respectable women whatever their class. This was reflected in neat, less elaborate hairstyles. Early photographs of the young Queen show her with the centre parting that was to remain fashionable until the 1860s, her front hair looped down over her ears and then back into a high, plaited bun. By the middle of the century some ladies were wearing their front hair in soft ringlets covering their ears and falling to the collar bones; many others wore more formal ringlets at the sides of the face and later these ringlets moved further towards the back of the head. Hair looped over the ears in plaited hoops was also popular. The

back hair remained dressed in a bun or soft chignon. In later years the influence of the Princess of Wales led to hair rising and the demise of the center parting in favor of a mass of soft curls on the forehead.

False hair was deemed out of fashion although many women wore false chignons and falls, a fact reflected in the value of pieces imported to Britain — £45,000 in 1865. The second highest importer was the United States. For evening, hair was decorated with ribbons and artificial flowers.

Victorian hairstyles are easy to recreate on medium-length or long hair. All you need is a center parting and some ringlets — you can either create these in your own hair or add false ones. The style on page 101 is best suited to medium-length hair and would require the addition of a false bun. Ideally you would use long hair to create the style on the left.

> **ALSO SEE**
>
> ❋ page 52: Attaching a false hairpiece
>
> ❋ page 54: Attaching ringlets

Victorian men

Under the influence of Prince Albert sobriety dominated men's fashion. The flamboyant dress sense of men such as Benjamin Disraeli and Charles Dickens was frowned upon in the 1840s. At the beginning of the century men were close-shaven and wore their hair short and brushed forward but soon the influence of Albert, with his side parting, short hair full at the sides of the head, and long whiskers (which eventually became a sort of under beard and walrus moustache), was seen everywhere. Some men wore their hair centrally parted with mutton chop whiskers and a moustache (or had no moustache at all). The Kaiser moustache also became a popular feature. Male hair was rarely worn below the ears until much later in the century. Then, with the Prince of Wales' influence at the center of high society, beards became fashionable once more.

This period is simple to achieve with short hair. You will need to grow a moustache and, if you can, long side whiskers. Otherwise you can use false pieces.

> **ALSO SEE**
>
> ❋ page 70: How to apply facial hairpieces securely
>
> ❋ page 71: Waxing moustaches

Kaiser moustache

Walrus moustache

The Edwardians ~ the late 1800s ~ 1910

Although Queen Victoria didn't die until 1901, the style we know as Edwardian was well established before that date, originating with the glittering court of the Prince and Princess of Wales, the hub of fashionable society. This means, for our purpose, that most of the important plays of the late 19th century are dressed in what we know as Edwardian style and not Victorian costume. Under the patronage of Edward VII as Prince of Wales and later King, theatre of all types flourished in England. Oscar Wilde's *The Importance of Being Earnest* and *An Ideal Husband* were huge successes and George Bernard Shaw had eleven of his plays produced at the Royal Court Theatre in London from 1904-7. Anton Chekhov's plays *The Three Sisters, Uncle Vanya, The Cherry Orchard* and *The Seagull* were written during this period, as was Henrik Ibsen's *Hedda Gabler*. Arthur Wing Pinero wrote *The Magistrate* and Gilbert and Sullivan continued their Savoy operas. Music Hall was still immensely popular and in America Burlesque continued to flourish as a breeding ground for later movie stars such as W. C. Fields. Other productions set in this period include *Hello Dolly* and, of course, *My Fair Lady*.

Edwardian women

This was the time of the mature beauty, a look which was so admired that young girls actually sought to look older in order to be fashionable. King Edward's preference for older, beautiful women and the rise of photography made some of these "professional beauties", like Lily Langtry, icons for ordinary women. Their images were sold on picture postcards and thus became widely available. The elegant and ever youthful Queen was herself an important influence and a leader of high society fashion. At this time hair was universally worn up, frequently with the addition of false chignons and curls.

There were two clearly defined styles. The first, favored by Alexandra, was worn flat to the head at the sides of the face and dressed high in elaborate curls, the back finished in a flattened chignon. The second popular style was copied from the work of the American artist Charles Dane Gibson and epitomized by "Gibson Girl" Camille Clifford on the London stage. This was much softer and fuller at the sides, smooth in appearance and culminated in a coiled bun on the crown of the head.

Unless you have plenty of hair and are good at handling it, these are difficult styles to do yourself. You will need to use rats to create the Gibson Girl hairdo. The Alexandra style would almost certainly require false pieces to be added to your own hair. In most productions with a halfway decent budget, wigs are usually provided for this period.

Gibson Girl style

ALSO SEE

❉ page 40: Edwardian Gibson Girl style

❉ page 52: Attaching a false hairpiece

Alexandra style

ALSO SEE

❊ page 70: How to apply facial hairpieces securely

Edwardian men

Although Edward VII was sixty when he finally became king, his influence as a leader of fashion was well established and he was known as one of the most stylish dressers of the day. He was extremely interested in both male and female fashion and personally gave his seal of approval to the Tyrolean hat and the Norfolk jacket but the thumbs down to the Panama hat. Initially he had copied the hair and facial styles of his father, Prince Albert, but by 1875 he was sporting a full beard trimmed to a soft point and a down-turned moustache — these were to be a key part of his look for the rest of his life. This style of beard and moustache was much copied in Edwardian society. However, gentlemen of a more artistic bent like Oscar Wilde, and aristocrats like Lord Ribblesdale and Winston Churchill were clean-shaven. Many men chose to grow moustaches and the upturned "Kaiser moustache" of Edward's nephew William II was also popular. Hair was generally short and worn brushed back behind the ears although there were exceptions to the rule as exemplified by the styles of Wilde and the politician Arthur Balfour.

All you need for plays of this period is a beard and moustache, either home-grown or false, and a neat short haircut.

The 1920s

This decade, also known as the Roaring Twenties, saw theatre challenged for the first time by the new medium of cinema.

During this time many artists who were destined to become major movie stars appeared in the West End, including Fred Astaire with his sister Adele in Gershwin's *Oh, Kay* and Paul Robeson as Eugene O'Neill's *Emperor Jones*. Also during this decade O'Neill gave us *Desire Under the Elms* and the Irish playwright Sean O'Casey premiered *Juno and the Paycock*. But the playwright of the decade has to be Noël Coward, who between 1920 and 1930 saw sixteen of his plays and revues produced on the London stage, including the controversial *The Vortex, Hay Fever, Bitter Sweet* and *This Year of Grace*. More recent productions set in this period include Sandy Wilson's *The Boy Friend,* Jerry Herman's *Mack and Mabel, Ma Rainey's Black Bottom* by August Wilson and Julie Styne's musical *Gypsy.*

1920s women

The new freedoms gained by women during the First World War benefited the Bright Young Things of the Jazz Age, who became known as "flappers". After horrific accidents in the munitions factories, the women who worked there cut the luxurious hairstyles of the Edwardian Era into ear-length bobs. This revolutionary change coincided with the invention of the Permanent Wave. The cloche hat came into fashion, which necessitated still neater and shorter hair, and the shingle style, with its soft front waves and short back, was developed. Still later, in 1925, the Eton crop, a very mannish style, became fashionable. Women wore these styles either smooth, marcel-waved with hot tongs into tight waves, or (if they could afford it) permanently waved. Later, hair lengthened to below the ears but remained in waves. Women who wished to keep their hair long dressed the front fashionably and wore the back in a chignon. The big influence on hairstyles during this decade

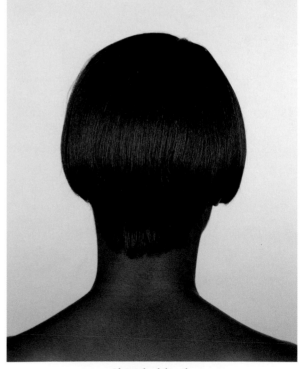
Shingled back

Shingled front

was Hollywood, and in England stars of the stage, like the glamorous Gertrude Lawrence, were widely admired.

These styles are relatively easy to reproduce with short hair. A marcelled look can be recreated by setting with pincurls. Longer hair could be waved at the front and taken back into a chignon. A false chignon could be added if you prefer.

> ### ALSO SEE
> ❋ page 27: Designing the pli for a hairstyle
> ❋ page 32: Pincurls — how to achieve the perfect curl
> ❋ page 53: Adding a false chignon

1920s men

I can hear a sigh of relief among my male readers as we come to this decade. The freedoms enjoyed by the flappers of the 1920s reached fashionable men as well. Clothes, although still relatively formal, became more comfortable, and beards and moustaches went out of fashion. Only older men still clung to the walrus moustache so familiar in photographs of the First World War. Hair was universally worn short, usually parted on one side and combed back off the face. Side whiskers were rarely seen, although some Hollywood stars of Latin descent, like Rudolf Valentino and Ramon Navarro, grew carefully shaved flat ones. Hair was kept in place with brilliantine and hair dressings.

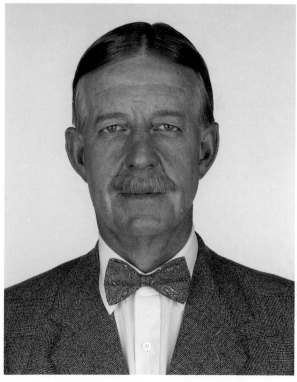

This is an easy period to recreate assuming that you don't have too many layers cut in your hair. Hair will need to be combed into a side parting and kept neat with a gel or wax (this will also give it shine).

The 1930s

The shock of the Depression and rumblings of political unrest in Europe blew away the excesses of the 1920s but theatre remained basically lighthearted. However, some writers like Frederico García Lorca, with his plays *Blood Wedding* and *The House of Bernardo Alba*, and Clifford Odets, who wrote *Golden Boy* and *Waiting for Lefty*, showed another side to society. In Great Britain The Shakespeare Memorial Theatre opened at Stratford-upon-Avon in 1935 and during this decade Thornton Wilder won the Pulitzer prize for drama with *Our Town*. The London stage saw J. B. Priestley's time plays *Dangerous Corner* and *Time and the Conways* produced and Noël Coward continued his success with his sparkling *Private Lives*. Broadway saw the opening of Gershwin's *Porgy and Bess*, Cole Porter's *Anything Goes* and Rodgers and Hart's *Babes in Arms*.

Other productions set in the 30s include George and Ira Gershwin's *Crazy for You* and *Grand Hotel* by Wright, Forrest and Yeston.

1930s women

Hollywood stars had a huge influence on fashion in the 30s especially after the invention of Technicolor® film. Once women could see the hair and make-up colors of the stars they demanded them for themselves. Greta Garbo's long bob and Marlene Dietrich's sophisticated styles were widely copied, as was Veronica Lake's long "peek-a-boo" hairstyle which partially covered one eye. When World War II was declared this style was such

a risk to her fans working in factories that she made a short propaganda film explaining that she didn't normally wear her hair like that. "Any girl who wears her hair over one eye is silly," she said, "I certainly don't, except in pictures." Another important influence during this time was the elegant Wallis Simpson, later Duchess of Windsor, with her dark, smooth hair drawn back in a chignon.

You will need to set your hair with rollers to create the soft waves of this era although generally wigs would be used for the really fashionable styles of the day.

ALSO SEE

❋ page 27: Designing the pli for a hairstyle

❋ page 30: Rollers — how to use them

❋ page 53: Adding a false chignon

❋ page 55: How to put on a hair lace wig

❋ page 67: False eyelashes

ALSO SEE

❋ page 44: Filling in a beard, moustache or side whiskers

1930s men

Sophistication was the key to men's fashion in the 30s and the source of this sophistication was Hollywood. The style set by movie stars such as Cary Grant and Fred Astaire influenced young men worldwide. The other important fashion icon at this time was the elegant Prince of Wales who continually made fashion headlines. During this period hair remained short with a side parting.

Moustaches, which were unfashionable in the 1920s, made a comeback due to the influence of film stars such as Ronald Coleman and William Powell. These were trimmed into small neat shapes, usually with a central gap. Beards were definitely unfashionable and side whiskers rarely seen.

This is a simple style to reproduce. You don't even need to grow a moustache — you can draw it.

The 1940s

1940-45 saw war in Europe, with the United States joining the Allies after the bombing of Pearl Harbor in 1941. As actors were conscripted or went to work in the munitions factories, London theatres went black. During this decade Tennessee Williams wrote two of his most important plays examining relationships, *The Glass Menagerie* and *A Streetcar Named Desire*, and Arthur Miller won the Pulitzer prize for *Death of a Salesman*. As theatre returned to normal in the West End, Noël Coward wrote the successful *Blithe Spirit* and Broadway staged the young Leonard Bernstein's *On the Town* and Rodgers and Hammerstein's *South Pacific*. Richard Rodgers had another Broadway success with Lorenz Hart when they wrote the racy *Pal Joey*. Also set in the 1940s are *Bent* by Martin Sherman, *City of Angels* by Coleman and Zippel, and Neil Simon's *Lost in Yonkers*.

1940s women

With the introduction of clothing coupons and the scarcity of fabric, the United Kingdom entered a period of "make do and mend" fashion-wise. To save material, skirts became shorter, and the fluid bias cut clothes of the 1930s gave way to styles influenced by military uniforms. Even silk stockings disappeared and, desperate for a little glamour, women all over Europe looked to Hollywood as inspiration for the one part of their bodies that

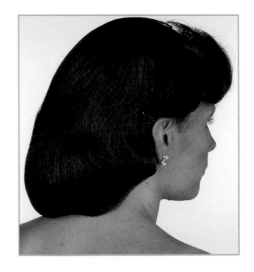

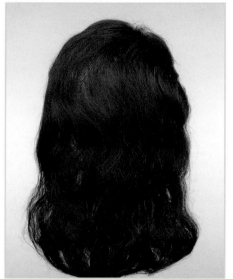

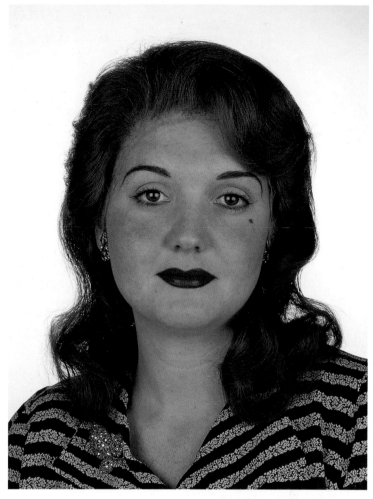

ALSO SEE

❋ page 27: Designing the pli for a hairstyle

❋ page 30: Rollers — how to use them

❋ page 41: 1940s rolled hairstyle

❋ page 52: Attaching a false hairpiece

❋ page 67: False eyelashes

remained untouched by restrictions — their hair. The short waved styles popularized by stars like Jean Harlow went out and in their place came long hair elaborately dressed in rolls and waves. It was worn up or down and the styles seen on stars like Bette Davis and the forces' pin-up Bette Grable, were widely copied. Women in the forces rolled the back of their hair up in a sausage shape which sat neatly below the back of their caps. For evening, hair was often decorated with black velvet bows or fresh flowers like camellias.

Short hair will definitely need a wig for this decade. Medium-length hair will need a hairpiece and long hair will require a good set, backcombing and plenty of hairspray.

1940s men

With most men in the services by 1941, the fashion in Europe and America was for very short hair. In England this was called a "short back and sides"; in the States the extremely short crew-cut appeared. The brave young pilots of the Royal Air Force, however, were permitted to wear their hair a little longer, and their use of a popular hair dressing of the day inspired the nickname "The Brylcreem Boys", greatly boosting sales of the product. During this decade most men were clean-shaven and side whiskers and beards were unusual.

Some senior military officers wore neat upturned moustaches and the odd handlebar style was worn. Two notable moustaches, those of General de Gaulle and Adolf Hitler, failed to make an influence on fashion.

This period requires a neat haircut with a strong side parting. You could grow a moustache like this or use a false one.

ALSO SEE

✳ page 70: How to apply facial hairpieces securely

The 1950s

As the world slowly recovered from war, theatre burst into life again. The English Stage Company was founded at London's Royal Court Theatre with the aim of promoting new plays. In 1956 it staged a production that was to change the face of English theatre — John Osborne's *Look Back in Anger*. The play marked a turning point in the history of theatre, bringing a whole new reality to drama. In this decade he also wrote *The Entertainer* which starred Laurence Olivier as the seedy Archie Rice. Meanwhile Terence Rattigan examined the quiet desperation of the middle classes in *Separate Tables* and Samuel Beckett wrote *Waiting for Godot*. Broadway audiences saw Arthur Miller's *A View from the Bridge* for the first time and Tennessee Williams' steamy *Cat on a Hot Tin Roof*. Leonard Bernstein wrote *Wonderful Town* and in collaboration with Stephen Sondheim created the wonderful musical *West Side Story*, which is set in New York but based on William Shakespeare's *Romeo and Juliet*.

Other shows set in this period include Shelagh Delaney's *A Taste of Honey*, Arnold Wesker's *Chips with Everything*, Reginald Ross's *Twelve Angry Men* and musicals *The Pajama Game* (by Richard Adler and Jerry Ross), *Damn Yankees* (by George Abbott and Douglas Wallop) and *Guys and Dolls* (by Frank Loesser).

1950s women

Europe was still recovering from the Second World War at the beginning of the 50s, with austerity and rationing still in place in Great Britain. But fashion had already moved on with the arrival of Christian Dior's New Look in 1947. Square-shouldered padded clothes gave way to huge, swirling skirts and tiny waists. Hollywood invented the Teenager who wore pedal pushers and extremely tight pencil skirts. The elaborate rolled hairstyles of the previous decade gave way to short hair, bubble cuts and the French pleat. Elegant women copied Grace Kelly's simple upswept hairstyle or Gina Lollobrigida's carefully set Italian boy hairdo. Young girls chose Audrey Hepburn's gamin cut or wore their hair in a high pony tail like the young Brigitte Bardot.

ALSO SEE

❋ page 27: Designing the pli for a hairstyle

❋ page 36: Creating a French pleat

❋ page 66: 1950s everyday fashion style

❋ page 67: False eyelashes

The 1950s has a hairstyle to suit every hair length: urchin cuts for short hair, more formal set styles for mid-length and the French pleat for longer hair. They are all achievable with a little practice and a good photograph to copy.

1950s men

During the 1950s fashion began to be dictated by young working class men for the first time. Their icons were James Dean and Elvis Presley. In response to the grayness of postwar Britain, "Teddy Boys" appeared — young men aping the fashions of Edwardian England with their velvet-collared drape jackets, drainpipe trousers and crêpe-soled shoes. Both British and American fans of Dean and Presley grew their hair long at the front with short sideburns and greased it back into a quiff. More conventional men wore their hair short and parted but no longer heavily greased. Fashion conscious men on both sides of the Atlantic were clean-shaven.

Any short hairstyle can be combed into a basic style of this decade but to achieve a good quiff the front hair will need to be long. Then you can backcomb it, add gel or wax to the surface of the hair and carefully smooth it back. Some men have thick hair which goes into a quiff without backcombing.

ALSO SEE

❋ page 34: Backcombing or teasing hair

The 1960s

The 1960s saw London become the focus of everything new and fashionable as its vibrant youth culture rocked the world. British theatre and its actors reaped benefits from this attention as London became the place to be. The New Realism of British theatre brought Harold Pinter to the fore with his plays *Homecoming, The Collection* and *The Caretaker*, and also Joe Orton with his outrageous *Entertaining Mr Sloane* and *Loot*. John Osborne wrote *Inadmissible Evidence* and Peter Shaffer's *Black Comedy* appeared. Broadway saw Tennessee Williams' *Suddenly Last Summer* and *Night of the Iguana* staged, and Edward Albee's *A Delicate Balance* and *Who's Afraid of Virginia Woolf?* were premiered in New York.

Other shows set in this period include Cy Coleman and Dorothy Field's *Sweet Charity*, the anti-war musical *Hair* by Ragni, Rado and McDermott, and Neil Simon's *The Odd Couple* and *Plaza Suite*.

1960s women

This was the time of mini skirts, hot pants and big make-up. The British designer Mary Quant dominated young fashion. Hollywood ceased to be influential as women copied the make-up and hairstyles of top models like Jean Shrimpton and later Twiggy. Wigs and hairpieces came back into fashion after forty years in the wilderness and false eyelashes, sometimes two pairs on the top lid and one under the eyes, became de rigueur. Initially hair was worn up, backcombed in high beehive styles, but then it became flattened on the top and coronets of false curls were added, often intertwined with flowers for parties. Switches and long hair attached to an Alice band sold well. As the decade progressed the heavy fringed geometric short cut created by Vidal Sassoon became very fashionable.

Beehives are easy to do if you have hair that is long or shoulder length. The Vidal Sassoon

cuts are usually best created by wigs unless you have a great hairdresser and thick hair. False eyelashes are an absolute must for the 1960s.

ALSO SEE

✻ page 34: Backcombing or teasing hair

✻ page 36: Creating a French pleat

✻ page 52: Attaching a false hairpiece

✻ page 67: False eyelashes

1960s men

At last men had a chance to shine again after several dull decades. Sharp Italian suits with shorter jackets and tapered trousers became fashionable, and even conservative men wore brightly colored "kipper" ties. The huge impact of The Beatles brought collarless suits and polo neck sweaters into fashion and their heavily fringed hairstyles influenced young trendy men everywhere. Men of all ages ceased to flatten their hair down and let it grow to collar length with short sideburns. The Rolling Stones created another image with their untidy hairstyles. Moustaches and beards were out of fashion until the end of the decade and the advent of Flower Power and the Hippie.

This is not a difficult period to recreate. Basically you need a haircut which comes to the collar at the back and short sideburns. Our model doesn't have a fringe so I have brushed his front hair forward and trimmed any long pieces (see page 117 to see him with a 1950s quiff — it's the same haircut).

Older or less fashionable men would have kept 1950s styles, perhaps grown a bit longer.

The 1970s

The 1970s saw youth strengthen its grip on society as a direct result of the growth of young people's spending power. Young directors and playwrights continued to influence theatre. Tom Stoppard's *Travesties* was produced in London as was David Storey's *Home*. His other Royal Court success *The Changing Room* was named Best Play of the Season by New York drama critics when it transferred there. Peter Shaffer wrote *Sleuth* and his play *Equus* opened to dramatic acclaim on Broadway. In the UK, Alan Ayckbourn produced the first of a long run of successes, *The Norman Conquests*. New York audiences saw Sondheim's *Company* and Michael Bennett won the Pulitzer prize in 1976 with *A Chorus Line*.

Among the many shows set in this decade are Neil Simon's *The Prisoner of Second Avenue*, Stoppard's *Travesties* and Mike Leigh's *Abigail's Party*.

1970s women

The 1970s were a time of confusion and disorder, and fashion reflected this. The Vietnam Flower Power protests in America made hippie and ethnic looks fashionable and pop stars like Janis Joplin and Jimi Hendrix espoused this street fashion. Hendrix's afro hairstyle, coming at the time of the Black is Beautiful campaign, was worn by millions of girls and men (me included!) as they permed their hair to full frizzy curls. Although pop stars were the new fashion icons, movie and television could still influence hairstyles. Many girls copied Lisa Minelli's gamin haircut in *Cabaret* and Farrah Fawcett Major influenced smarter women with her flicked back look. When Bo Derek appeared in the film *10* with her long blond hair dressed into tiny African plaits, it spawned a million look-a-likes.

You can really take your choice in this period as it was the beginning of a variety of different looks. You will need to research to find what is right for your character. Many younger women

ALSO SEE

❊ page 34: Backcombing or teasing hair

❊ page 64 to see a department store fashion wig in a typical 1970s 'big hair' style

just grew their hair long and wore it naturally, usually with a fringe. Older women often still wore more formal, backcombed styles.

1970s men

At this time the division between younger and older men became much more noticeable in fashion terms. Older men still clung to their suits, albeit now with flared trousers and worn with shirts with long, pointed collars. Younger men took to the more relaxed ethnic and hippie fashions which mixed and matched styles in a somewhat chaotic way and even, for a time, wore beads. The Beatles now had hair down to their collars and beyond with long Edwardian side whiskers and the front brushed casually forward. To this they added the highly popular turned down moustache made fashionable by Che Guevara. John Lennon was to go still further and grow his hair below his shoulders and parted in the center, adding a natural beard. Conventional men were influenced too and they grew their hair to collar length with side whiskers and added thick moustaches.

Some younger men grew their hair and had it permed into afro styles or let it grow as long as possible, adding thick side whiskers. Pop star Marc Bolan of T. Rex was a riot of dark cherubic curls but completely clean-shaven. Depending on your character you might have long hair for this period. You would certainly have a moustache, side whiskers and possibly also a beard. You need to research to decide which look would be appropriate. Family photo albums are great for researching this period but try not to laugh!

ALSO SEE

❊ page 55: How to put on a hair lace wig

❊ page 58: How to put on a stretch-base wig

❊ page 70: How to apply facial hairpieces securely

A final word . . .

Well, here we are at the end of the book. I hope you have enjoyed what you have read and will feel much more confident, indeed inspired, when handling real and artificial hair in the future.

Most of the Key Tools I have mentioned are to be found in larger pharmacies, department stores and hairdresser suppliers. The more specialist products, for example, spirit gum and toupee tape, can be bought at theatrical stockists like those listed below. Real hair wigs can be hired and purchased from wig specialists such as Derek Easton who supplied the wigs we used in this book.

I wish you good luck and great productions!

Stockists

UK

Charles H Fox Ltd
22 Tavistock Street
London WC2E 7PY

Screenface
24 Powis Terrace
London W11 1JH

Derek Easton Hair
& Wigs
Studio on 2nd Avenue
Kingsway Court
Queens Gardens
Hove
East Sussex BN3 2LR

USA

Kryolan Corporation
132 Ninth Street
San Francisco
California
CA 94103

Bob Kelly Cosmetics
151 West 46th Street
New York
NY 10036

Bibliography

Angeloglou, Maggie, *A History of Make-Up*, Studio Vista, 1970

Best, Geoffrey, *Mid Victorian Britain 1851-75*, Fontana Press, 1971

Blum, Daniel, *A Pictorial History of the Talkies*, Spring Books, 1958

Burke, John, *An Illustrated History Of England*, Book Club Associates, 1974

Corson, Richard, *Stage Make-Up*, Prentice-Hall Inc., 1975

Falkus, Christopher, *The Life and Times of Charles II*, George Weidenfeld & Nicholson and Book Club Associates, 1972

Gemsheim, Alison, *Victorian & Edwardian Fashion — A Photographic Survey*, Dover Publications Inc., 1981

Griffith, Richard & Marpet, Arthur, *The Movies*, Bonanza Books, 1957

Grum. Bernard, *Timetables of History,* Simon & Schuster 1991

Houri, Peter, *Working The Halls*, Futura Publications, 1974

Keenan, Bridget, *The Women We Wanted To Look Like*, St. Martins Press Inc., 1978

Laver, James, *Costume and Fashion*, Thames and Hudson, revised 1995

Legrand, Jacques, *Chronicle of the 20th Century*, Chronicle Communications

Madden, Grant & Nicholas, *The Countryside at War*, Jupiter Books (London) Ltd, 1975

Middlemas, Keith, *The Life and Times of Edward VII*, George Weidenfeld & Nicholson and Book Club Associates, 1972

Mitford, Nancy, *Madame De Pompadour,* Hamish & Hamilton, 1954

Nunn, Joan, *Fashions in Costume 1200-1980,* The Herbert Press, 1984

Swinfield, Rosemarie, *Period Make-Up for the Stage*, A & C Black Ltd, 1997

Trewin, J.C., *The Gay Twenties*, Macdonald & Co., 1958

Vickers, Hugo, *Cecil Beaton*, George Weidenfeld & Nicholson Ltd, 1985

Williams, Neville, *The Life and Times of Elizabeth I*, George Weidenfeld & Nicholson and Book Club Associates, 1972

Woodforde, John, *The Strange Story of False Hair*, Routledge & Keenan Paul, 1971

Glossary

Backcombing/teasing Combing method for adding volume and height to hairstyles.

Bald cap Latex or plastic head cover used to simulate baldness.

Beard stubble stick Wax adhesive stick rubbed on the chin to attach tiny pieces of crêpe hair.

Bob Short female hairstyle popular in the 1920s and 1960s.

Brilliantine Lotion for dressing and adding shine to short male hairstyles.

Brylcreem Famous male hair cream immortalized by its association with the British pilots of the Second World War who became known as "The Brylcreem Boys".

Bubble cut Short and very curly female hairstyle, popular in the 1950s.

Bun ring Circle of crêpe hair or other material, used to support a bun at the back of a woman's head.

Cake make-up Theatrical water-based foundation sold in many colors.

Chignon Coil of hair, usually worn at the nape of the neck but sometimes worn higher.

Crêpe hair Inexpensive false hair sold by the yard or meter in narrow plaits.

Crew-cut Short, blunt cut American male hairstyle.

Eton crop Masculine hairstyle worn by some fashionable women during the 1920s.

French pleat Elegant way of folding and putting up longer hair.

Gamin cut Short flicked cut popularized in the 1950s by stars like Audrey Hepburn.

Gibson Girl Idealized woman created by American painter Charles Dance Gibson and widely copied by fashionable women in the time of Edward VII, both in the United Kingdom and the United States.

Hair lace Net on which real hair is knotted to create wigs and facial hairpieces.

Hair thickener Product which coats hair follicles, giving the appearance of a thicker head of hair.

Half-wig A wig which hides baldness at the front of the head.

Handlebar moustache A large moustache with curled ends.

Kaiser moustache Moustache with pointed upturned ends made popular by Kaiser William II of Prussia during the late Victorian and Edwardian periods.

Marcel wave Method of using heated tongs to create tight little waves, which was popular in the 1920s.

Moustache wax Soft wax for shaping moustaches.

Permanent wave Full name for "perm", a method of using chemicals to create lasting curls in the hair.

Pincurls Small pieces of curled hair used to create styles.

Pli The setting pattern of a hairstyle.

Queue Small tail of hair at the back of 18th century wigs.

Quiff A section of hair brushed up, and sometimes out, above the forehead.

Rat Shaped piece of wadding used under elaborate hairstyles for support.

Ringlets Long vertical curls, usually worn in clusters.

Shingle style Short, close-fitting 1920s female hairstyle.

Spirit gum Theatrical liquid adhesive used to stick wigs, bald caps and facial hair to the skin.

Toupee Small hairpiece used to hide a receding hairline.

Toupee tape Theatrical double-sided tape which secures toupees and half-wigs to bare skin.

Urchin cut Short, boyish female hairstyle.

Walrus moustache Large moustache with drooping ends.

Wig block Wooden or polystyrene head shape on which a wig can be placed for styling or safe keeping.

Wig clamp Metal or wooden spike which can be clamped to a table to support a wig block.

Wig spring Tiny coiled spring which can be attached to short hair to provide a means of securing a wig.

Index

125

128